Judith Wills is one of the UK's best-known and knowledge-able nutrition and diet experts, with the knack of making a healthy lifestyle both fun and accessible. She has sold over two million copies of her books worldwide, including the international bestseller *The Food Bible*. Her books have been translated into more than twenty languages across the world and have appeared in the bestseller lists in most countries.

Judith's twenty years' experience in the health, diet and nutrition field coupled with her own life as a working mother give her a special insight into the problems of all the family in attempting to stay fit and healthy. She lives in an old vicarage on the borders of Herefordshire and Wales with her husband and younger son.

By the same author

The Diet Bible
The Children's Food Bible
The Food Bible
Slim for Life
Six Ways to Lose a Stone in Six Weeks
The Omega Diet
Judith Wills' Slimmers Cookbook
Judith Wills' Virtually Vegetarian

THE →→→→→
TRAFFIC LIGHT
→→→→→ DIET

JUDITH WILLS

ORION

An Orion Paperback
First published in Great Britain in 2004 by
Orion Books Ltd,
Orion House, 5 Upper St Martin's Lane,
London WC2H 9EA

A CIP catalogue record for this book
is available from the British Library.

ISBN: 0 75286 445 9

Printed and bound in Great Britain by
Clays Ltd, St Ives plc

CONTENTS

WHY THE TRAFFIC LIGHT DIET?

When I wrote my last 'diet book' about five years ago, I felt at the time that I would not be writing another, as there was little new left to say, in the narrow world of slimming and weight control, that was also healthy, truthful and workable.

Why am I now introducing the Traffic Light Diet to you? Because I realised early one morning last summer that this system, this simple and easy way of dieting – while based on well-documented concepts in the way of nutritional research – is so good, so workable and so very user-friendly that it needed to be brought together for anyone who has had trouble sticking to diets in the past.

In fact, the Traffic Light system is one that I have recommended several times over the past few years. I outlined it in *The Food Bible* and *The Diet Bible*, and have put several would-be slimmers on to a similar programme from time to time with great results.

The idea of presenting the Traffic Light system in a paperback format occurred to me that morning because I had just read the newly published and important Commons Select Committee report, titled *Obesity*. This had been written with the aim of pointing the government in the right direction in helping the rest of us to fight and beat the growing problem in the UK, where now approximately two-thirds of adults are overweight and a third are actually clinically obese.

It seemed to me that the core of the report was the Committee's recommendation that a traffic light system of food labelling should be introduced to help consumers make sensible, calorie-controlling choices when they purchase food and drink. It also reminded me of just how great the Traffic Light slimming system is, because it is so, so easy for everyone to follow.

Hence this book – which also, incidentally, takes on board all the other main weight-control recommendations within the same report, including ideas for exercise. Throughout the book, any quotes you find in italics are taken from the Select Committee report.

So what is the Traffic Light Diet all about?

Well, it really is the most simple diet ever. It is also healthy and balanced, with no reliance on restricting important food groups such as carbs, proteins or essential fats. It is suitable for almost everyone over the age of five, as whatever your own preferences and lifestyle, you can make it work for *you*.

And work it will.

You just choose *most* of your foods from the 'GREEN for go – eat as much as you like' lists; *some* of your foods from the 'AMBER – go carefully' lists; and finally just a *few* (or very small portions of) foods from the 'RED – stop and think' lists.

Chapter 1 will explain in more detail just why this is such a brilliant system – but that, really, is all you need to know to start following the diet. Once you know which foods come into which category, there is nothing else you need to do in order to lose weight steadily and keep it off – apart, of course, from upping your activity levels a little.

I make no apologies for the simplicity of this diet, or for the fact that I am not plugging anything weird while trying to convince you how wonderful it is. This plan is not a gimmick – it just promotes healthy weight loss with no hassle ... and what more can any overweight person want?

Judith Wills
September 2004

LOSE WEIGHT THE TRAFFIC LIGHT WAY

Isn't it about time we stopped falling for each new fad diet that comes along and started losing weight, and then maintaining a sensible weight, in a rational manner?

Isn't it about time we ditched the low-carbs, the carb-frees, the fat-frees, the 'don't mix your proteins and your carbs', the 'liquids only' or 'raw only' or 'soup only' crazy diets and came of age about slimming?

A few years ago I vowed I wouldn't write another paperback diet book because they have such a bad name, and no wonder. But when the recent *Obesity* report was published, I had one of those 'click' moments when I realised that I really, really wanted to bring the oh-so-simple Traffic Light slimming system to you – because it *isn't* a fad diet, it isn't silly, it isn't unbalanced and, above all, it is easy to both follow and stick to.

Because the fad diets get lots of publicity, sensible ones like the Traffic Light Diet don't get the attention they deserve. I sincerely hope this book is the exception because it is a system I can wholeheartedly recommend as the best and healthiest way to lose weight and keep it off.

Although the Traffic Light Diet is easy to follow and simple in concept, it is by no means a one-trick pony but offers a variety of benefits. Of course it provides an almost failsafe way of losing weight without bother or discomfort. But it also effortlessly embraces all the accepted guidelines for healthy eating and will therefore perhaps provide you with an increase in well-being and immunity from disease.

It is a plan that can be used not just for a few weeks or months, but for life to maintain a healthy weight – and it is suitable for children over five as well as adults.

Chapter 1 examines all the ways that the Traffic Light Diet helps you to look and feel better, and also explains how important regular activity is to get the most from the plan.

Traffic Light for EASY Weight Loss

'Consumers need a simple system for choosing foods to make up a balanced diet.'

And the Traffic Light Diet really couldn't be simpler!

'Some foods should only be eaten in moderation by most people, and we therefore recommend a traffic light system which should be based on energy density. This would apply to all foods and will make it easier for consumers to make choices.'

The Traffic Light Diet offers the first full description of a workable traffic light plan. It takes on board this advice plus the Commons Select Committee's other main recommendations.

I know that the system works well for most people who try it, because over the past few years I have chosen to recommend it to several people who have wanted a diet that doesn't involve too much time or thought and who hate to do more than minimal calculation. In fact, the Traffic Light plan offers ways around virtually all of the main complaints that people have about diets and dieting, allowing you to fit it around your own likes, dislikes and lifestyle.

And this, surely, is the crux of a good diet. If you can follow it easily, you can stick to it. If you find it doesn't impinge on, or disrupt, your life too much, you can stick to it. Here are the main ways that the Traffic Light Diet *doesn't* ruin your life:

It's user-friendly

All you have to do is remember the basic three colour groups – GREEN, AMBER and RED – and what each means:

GREEN for Go – eat as much as you like!
AMBER for 'Go Carefully' – eat moderate amounts.
RED for 'Stop and Think' – avoid, eat only occasionally, or eat in very small quantities.

That's all there is to it. There is virtually no weighing or measuring of portions, so no need to keep getting out scales or calculators, and there is positively no calorie counting required – the Traffic Light system takes care of your calorie intake for you.

It is easy to prepare meals and snacks for yourself, family and friends from the GREEN and AMBER food lists so you don't have to get used to different shopping regimes or cooking methods.

You don't have to give up any food groups

If you have tried very low-fat diets or low-carbohydrate diets in the past, you will probably agree that, sooner or later, giving up one whole food group (the main ones are carbohydrates, proteins and fats) makes life very monotonous. On such diets it is hard to create interesting, balanced meals from a limited range of items.

More and more die-hard, high-protein diet fans are admitting that they could kill for a sandwich or a plate of pasta. Eventually they reach a point where they have to give up the regime. But a very low-fat diet isn't the answer either; it can prove to be extremely difficult to stick to as it involves major changes in the way you shop, prepare food and cook. On top of this, it is no more healthy than a high-protein diet.

Even more pertinent, perhaps, all the major research trials that have been undertaken in recent years show that, long term, the best way to lose weight and keep it off *is* on a balanced diet, high in carbohydrate, moderately low in fat (particularly saturated and trans fats) and containing adequate protein and fruit. As recently as July 2004 research published in the *American Journal of Clinical Nutrition* backed this up yet again.

On the Traffic Light Diet, you will be eating in exactly that way, from a wide variety of healthy and tasty foods.

No hunger pangs

One thing that most slimmers dread are those hunger pangs, and feeling hungry is one of the main reasons that they give up on diets. Bedtime, and you've used up all your day's calorie allowance? Nowhere near suppertime, and you're starving? Times like that just don't occur on this plan because you can always have something to eat. And, because the Traffic Light Diet contains adequate complex carbohydrates (most of which are low on the glycaemic index – see pages 15-16) and adequate protein and fat (which both act to keep hunger pangs at bay because they take longer to digest than carbohydrates), you tend to be able to survive for longer without getting hungry anyway.

Lastly, weight loss on the Traffic Light Diet is steady rather than rapid, which in itself helps to prevent hunger.

No depression

Lastly, because you can 'eat your fill' of GREEN foods, your plate need never look stingy – it can always be full. So you will feel better about sitting down to your 'slimmer's' meal.

Also, as your full plate will take you as long to eat as did your old, pre-dieting plateful, you won't face that sad scenario where you wolf down your mini-meal in a minute and sit there wondering how on earth you will last out until the next mealtime. In psychological terms, the diet has benefits, helping you to avoid diet depression and deprivation. No diet will be adhered to if you find it boring, mean, or unpleasant. Food, after all, should be a pleasure and something we look forward to. Take that away (as many diets do) and no wonder the calorie-reducing regime gets ditched.

Research shows that a high percentage of people 'yo-yo' diet – they lose a little weight, then get disillusioned, drop the diet and put all the weight back on. Next time, mentally, it is much harder to begin again. The Traffic Light Diet helps to prevent this yo-yoing as it encourages you to eat well and sensibly.

No banned foods

Although, in the RED section, I make personal recommendations that you should consider completely avoiding just a handful of food/drink items (and I give you my scientifically based reasons for these), in fact no food nor drink is completely banned on this diet. RED – 'Stop and Think' items are those you should eat infrequently, or in very small portions. Guidelines for interpreting this appear in the charts in Chapter 6. So if there is something that you are particularly keen to include in your diet, you can.

From alcohol to crisps to cake or cream, you don't have to say goodbye to your favourite for ever. However, in my experience, when you have been following the diet for a few weeks you will find that your tastebuds alter and that the previously desired items often just don't appeal so much any more.

It's a 'go-anywhere' diet

Because you can choose from such a wide range of foods, you will find that you don't have the same problems as do slimmers on many other diets when they are out and about – in restaurants, abroad and so on. You can virtually always find a meal that fits in with your diet.

And because you only have to know what's GREEN, what's AMBER and what's RED, it is easy to pick the right meals and snacks without recourse to a calculator.

Out shopping, life is easy too. All the GREEN and AMBER foods are widely and easily available, and you don't have to shop armed with calculator and charts.

It is not expensive

Unlike some diets, including a high-protein plan, you don't have to spend a fortune either. Many of the GREEN and AMBER foods are low in cost and the diet should actually save you money, as many of the foods in the RED section *are* quite expensive when you work out a 'weight per penny' ratio.

For example, a packet of crisps (RED) weighing about 35g (just over an ounce) will cost around 25p, so you are paying nearly 1p per gram of food. Whereas an apple (GREEN), weighing around 125g, costs around 25p and you are paying just one fifth of 1p per gram of food. Plus, of course, the apple contains a wider range of nutrients, and fewer calories by far, than the crisps. So if you also worked out a 'nutrients per penny' ratio, the GREEN and AMBER items on the Traffic Light Diet would win on that score too.

It's suitable for all the family

All dieting and non-dieting members of the family over five

years old can eat the Traffic Light way. This is a major bonus for all busy parents as there is nothing worse than having to prepare one set of meals for yourself and another for other family members.

The reason that the diet is suitable for all is that it is so adaptable, as well as being healthy, and it won't cause health or nutritional problems for other family members. Because you are eating 'normal' food, you shouldn't get a lot of complaints and refusals either.

The recipes in Chapter 5 will give you ideas for preparing tasty satisfying dishes and the menu plans in Chapter 3 will show you how to incorporate the recipes, and your own dishes, into a weekly diet.

For more information on others in the family and for non-dieters, see 'Your Questions Answered' in Chapter 4.

So, as you can see already, on so many levels this really is a hard diet plan to beat.

It is the one diet that doesn't take over your life – it just works.

Traffic Light for HEALTHY Weight Loss

Over the past years, the food industry – one of the country's most powerful and vocal collection of companies – has worked hard to get across a message that 'junk' food doesn't exist. However, the *Obesity* report has this to say:

'The food industry has made constant use of the argument that there are no such things as unhealthy foods, only unhealthy diets, but it is patently apparent that certain foods are hugely calorific in relation to their weight and/or their nutritional value compared to others.

'There are definitely foods we need to be eating less of and foods we need to be eating more of. A small amount of the [junk] foods – or these foods on an irregular basis – will not

particularly harm you in themselves. It is the degree of frequency and the size of the portions that is the issue.'

That is why the Committee recommends the Traffic Light system of weight loss. It not only provides an easy way to lose weight but also, happily, results in a diet that has a near-perfect balance of foods, which should naturally result in a healthier overall diet.

My Traffic Light plan works to improve the nutritional profile of your diet by limiting portion size and frequency of eating RED foods (which are not only high in calories but also of low nutritional value – sometimes called 'junk') while allowing unlimited use of GREEN foods and drinks (which are low in calories but with a high nutrient profile), and encouraging moderate use of AMBER foods or drinks (which are high or fairly high in calories but also have high nutritional value).

This sometimes means that a high-calorie food will not necessarily be in the RED group, because it is also inherently healthy with much to offer in the way of nutrients. Nuts and seeds are a good example. On many diets they are banned because they are high in calories compared with many other foods. But on the Traffic Light Diet they are allowed, because they contain many important elements, including unsaturated fatty acids and vitamin E among others.

To summarise ways in which the Traffic Light Diet ensures you have a healthy diet:

→ You can eat freely of all foods that have a high-nutrient/low or moderate calorie ratio (GREEN).
→ You eat regularly, in moderation, all foods that have a high-nutrient/high-calorie ratio (AMBER).
→ Your intake of all foods with a low-nutrient/high-calorie ratio is severely limited (RED).

There is a fourth group of 'foods', which have a low nutrient value, or potential negative health aspects, but which aren't in themselves high in calories. It includes items such as salt (sodium) or low-calorie diet drinks. I have grouped these with the RED foods, thus further improving the nutritional profile of the Traffic Light Diet .

This system is explained in more detail in Chapter 2. In the meantime here are the main ways in which eating on the Traffic Light Diet may help you to improved health and protection from disease:

It cuts total fat, saturated fat and trans fat intake

The diet helps you to reduce your total fat intake, mainly by reducing the amount of saturated fats (found in highest quantities in foods such as full-fat dairy produce, meat, pastries and other baked goods) and trans fats (found in highest quantities in commercial products such as pastries, hard fats, cakes and biscuits), while ensuring that your intake of the 'healthy' fats – the 'long-chain' polyunsaturated fatty acids such as the omega-3 group and the monounsaturated fats such as olive oil – remains intact or may even increase.

The links between your health and the amount – and type – of fat that you eat are many and well documented.

A **total fat** intake of more than 30–35 per cent of total calories is linked with an increased risk of heart disease and obesity. Obesity in itself is a risk factor for heart disease and many other ailments. The national total fat intake is currently around 38 per cent of total calorie intake.

Most of us eat too much **saturated fat**. The national average is that it accounts for around 15 per cent of total calories, whereas for health, around 10–11 per cent would be better, according to the Food Standards Agency and other health organisations.

Eating less total fat *and* less saturated fat would, the FSA says, lead to lower levels in the blood of total cholesterol as well as LDL cholesterol. (This is the type sometimes termed 'bad' cholesterol.) A high level of both total cholesterol and LDL cholesterol is closely related to the risk of heart disease.

Trans fats may be formed when liquid fats are converted into solid fats in a process known as 'hydrogenation', which is much used within the food industry. The end result is hydrogenated vegetable oil (fat), which may contain trans fats. These trans fats, it is now thought, may be more harmful to our health than saturated fats, and they have no nutritional benefits. They may, for instance, make our arteries more rigid (and we may therefore be more susceptible to stroke, for example) and they may be linked to adult-onset diabetes and childhood asthma. We should therefore try to avoid trans fats in the diet and certainly eat no more than 5g a day, although some experts feel that even this amount is too high.

Cutting back on saturates and trans fats will enable us to eat reasonable amounts of the **unsaturated** fats – **polyunsaturates** and **monounsaturates** – while still reducing our total fat intake.

Polyunsaturated fats tend to help lower blood LDL cholesterol levels and come into two categories, the omega-6s (N6s) and omega-3s (N3s). Most of us already eat plenty of polyunsaturates in the form of omega-6s – oils such as safflower, sunflower and corn. Indeed, a very high intake of these may not be a good idea, as they can oxidise in the body, causing potentially harmful 'free radicals' to be produced. Because oxidisation increases with heat, oils very high in polyunsaturates shouldn't be used too often in cooking at high temperatures. To help avoid oxidisation, vitamin E intake should also be increased. The omega-6 oils are classed as 'pro-inflammatory', meaning that a high intake may increase the risk of inflammatory diseases. So we need reasonable amounts of good-quality omega-6s, but too much is to be avoided – and recent research shows that omega-6 intake may be very high in some people, including children.

But many of us don't eat enough of the other type of polyunsaturated fats – the omega-3s. These are found in highest quantities in flaxseeds and flaxseed oil, walnut oil and rapeseed oil, and in smaller amounts in many other plant foods such as dark green leafy vegetables. Oily fish such as mackerel, herring, salmon, tuna, trout and sardines are rich in two particular types of omega-3, EPA and DHA. It is known that these omega-3 oils are anti-inflammatory and may have a wide range of benefits to health, including prevention or control of heart disease, some cancers, immune system deficiencies, arthritis, skin complaints and even Alzheimer's. Indeed, low omega-3 intake coupled with high omega-6 intake may explain the huge increase in asthma and allergies among our children over the past several years.

Many experts, including the British Nutrition Foundation, feel that it is important to alter the balance of our polyunsaturated fat intakes to increase the omega-3s and reduce the omega-6s.

And it is also worth remembering that a diet low in saturated and trans fats allows the beneficial omega-3 fats to do their work in the body, not only helping to prevent disease but also increasing brain power, concentration and learning capacity.

Monounsaturated fats, found in greatest amounts in olive oil, rapeseed oil, groundnut oil, some other nut oils and some nuts and seeds, tend to reduce LDL cholesterol and may raise 'good' HDL cholesterol in the blood. A diet rich in monounsaturates is linked with lower heart disease rates and may be an important component of the healthy 'Mediterranean'-type diet. Indeed, lightly processed ('cold pressed') olive oil also contains high levels of anti-oxidant plant chemicals, including squalene, which have been shown to protect the body from damaging free-radical compounds and may help to protect against some cancers. One further benefit of oils high in monounsaturates is that they are less prone to oxidation (which occurs when they are subjected to heat, light and long storage), making them the oils of choice for cooking and for the larder.

In conclusion, it seems fair to say that your diet should contain a mix of different fats and oils, including both omega-3 and omega-6, as well as oils high in monounsaturates – and that all the oil that you buy should be of top quality, preferably from first pressings, and you should store it away from heat and light to protect its composition and avoid oxidation. And a little 'natural' saturated fat, such as butter or the fat in meat, is almost certainly better for you than fat spreads and other items that contain trans fats.

Foods that contain high levels of 'good fats' should be cooked sympathetically, rather than overdone or burnt, which encourages oxidation and negates any beneficial effects.

The Traffic Light Diet helps you to choose a healthy mix of fats in reasonable amounts, with the accent on natural fats from good, wholesome, unadulterated food sources.

It cuts your sugar and refined carbohydrate intake

'Lowering the fat content of foods would not achieve the objective of reducing obesity if food manufacturers substitute fat with other high density foods such as refined carbohydrates and sugars. Energy density needs to be targeted, rather than just fat.'

Sugar is the only type of carbohydrate food for which the UK Department of Health has set an upper limit on consumption. It recommends that no more than 10 per cent of our daily calories should be in the form of sugars, of the type described as 'extrinsic'. This means sugars that aren't bound into the cellular structure of the food in which they are present.

Extrinsic sugars are found, for example, in all refined sugars, honey and treacle, in fruit squashes, fruit drinks, fizzy drinks, cakes, biscuits, chocolate, jams, confectionery, puddings and desserts that contain added sugar – and even in fruit juices.

At the moment we are eating nearly 20 per cent of our daily calories in the form of extrinsic sugars, up to double the recommended maximum. Research shows that a diet high in extrinsic sugars is linked with obesity and dental caries, and may even affect memory. Also, as sugar contains few or no nutrients except calories, people who regularly eat sugary foods in preference to high-nutrient foods may suffer from nutritional deficiencies.

Eating or drinking sugary produce – and highly refined cereal foods – can also play havoc with the level of sugar in your blood because such foods tend to be high on the glycaemic index. The G.I. Index is a table which ranks carbohydrate foods by how rapidly they raise blood sugar levels. It was originally designed to help diabetics control their blood sugars and therefore insulin release. In non-diabetics, a high intake of high G.I. foods may eventually cause insulin resistance, a pre-diabetic state. In a healthy body, insulin is produced to carry sugar from the blood to be used as energy in the body cells or to be stored as fat. But if sugar intake is consistently high, it may take more and more insulin to achieve this. Eventually the insulin response may become 'worn out' and no longer be efficient at removing sugar from the blood. This 'insulin resistance' is often a precursor to diabetes; it forms part of the group of symptoms known as 'Syndrome X' (the others are abdominal obesity, high blood pressure and a poor blood fats profile) which is linked with increased risk of heart disease and other problems.

The Traffic Light Diet cuts your intake of extrinsic sugars right back to well below the 10 per cent level, with most foods and drinks high in them on the RED list. There are a few on my list of foods that you should try to avoid altogether.

However, the Traffic Light Diet does allow you to eat, either freely or moderately, foods that contain 'intrinsic' sugars – i.e., sugars that form part of the natural cellular structure of the food. These foods include fresh and dried fruits, and, to a lesser extent, some vegetables, grains, pulses, nuts and seeds. The sugar in milk and dairy produce (lactose) is classed with the intrinsic sugars as, nutritionally, it is a natural part of an important food. All these foods that contain natural sugars are nutritious and form an important part of a balanced diet. While the Traffic Light Diet is *not* a 'Glycaemic Index Diet' (a diet based only on foods low on the G.I. Index) it does tend to naturally keep the blood sugar levels even, because it is naturally low in highly commercial refined and sugary foods. The Food Charts (see pp 166–224) provide more information on individual foods and their effects on blood sugar levels where I have considered it relevant.

It cuts your salt intake

A diet high in sodium is linked with an increase in blood pressure, which increases the risk of strokes and heart attacks. While we all need a small amount of sodium for good health because it helps to regulate fluid levels in the body and has other functions, in the UK we currently eat, on average, a lot more than we need.

Our average daily intake of sodium is around 3.6g, or 9g of salt (salt is 40 per cent sodium and 60 per cent chloride), while the UK Department of Health advises that we should eat no more than 2.4g sodium (6g salt). The World Health Organisation recommends a daily maximum of only 5g salt.

Our children should eat even less sodium. For example, four- to six-year-olds should have no more than 3g of salt a day or 1.2g sodium.

Sodium appears in high levels in many more of our foods than you might think, and in items that may surprise you. It is present not only in typically 'salty' foods such as table salt, crisps, salted nuts and bacon but also occurs in relatively large amounts in items such as bread, soups, meat products, breakfast cereals and many other processed products.

Indeed, it is estimated that 75 per cent of our salt intake comes from processed foods. The remainder comes mostly from salt added in cooking and at the table, and just a small amount comes from the sodium found naturally in basic foodstuffs.

The Traffic Light Diet helps you to reduce your salt intake by encouraging you to eat more of the less-processed foods and by including many of the highest-salt foods in the RED group.

In addition to this, you can help reduce the sodium content of your diet further by not adding salt to your cooking water or to food at the table; by choosing 'low-salt', 'reduced-salt' or 'salt-free' varieties of processed foods such as baked beans, bacon, stock cubes, crackers and cereals; and by avoiding canned products in brine (e.g. tuna, vegetables).

In the wake of a recent government report on salt in the diet, many food companies are actually taking steps to reduce the sodium content of their products so in time it should become easier and easier to eat less salt.

Tip

As a general rule, 0.5g sodium per 100g food is considered a lot of sodium, while 0.1g sodium per 100g food is considered a small amount. If you bear this in mind when shopping, it makes it easier to choose products that will help you reduce your total salt intake.

Remember that sodium and salt are not the same thing. When a manufacturer indicates the amount of sodium in a food, the actual salt content is 2.5 times greater. The daily level for adults to aim for is 2.5g sodium or 6g salt.

It helps you reduce the amount of artificial additives in your diet

A healthy diet is not simply one that cuts down on saturated fat and sugar, for example, or one that provides the complete range of nutrients. It is becoming clear that a diet high in the artificial additives that have become commonplace in processed foods over the past years may also be less than optimum.

Recent research has linked certain 'E' numbers with behavioural problems in children, allergies and asthma. And the Food Commission found that those foods containing the most additives are likely to have the poorest nutritional profile – in other words, they are more likely to be high in fat, sugar and salt.

The Traffic Light Diet helps you and your family to cut back on artificial colourants and flavourings in your diet by encouraging you to eat more naturally. The items in the RED group are most often high in additives while those in the GREEN group are least likely to be high in additives.

Tip
You can help reduce the additive content of your diet further by choosing wisely when you shop – for example, by choosing 'natural' smoked haddock or salmon rather than fish coloured with 'E' numbers, and by buying organic foods when you can afford it, which tend to contain fewer additives than non-organic brands.

It provides a nutritionally balanced diet

Because the Traffic Light Diet is a sensible plan (in that it encourages you to eat from a wide range of foods; it doesn't ban certain food groups (e.g. carbohydrates or fats); it doesn't want you to reduce your energy (calorie) intake too low; and yet it helps you to cut back on saturated fat, trans fats, sugar and salt), it offers you an almost impeccable diet, from a nutritional point of view.

You will be receiving all the vitamins, minerals, plant chemicals, fibre, protein, carbohydrate and essential fats that you and your family need for good health in the short and long term. Eating the Traffic Light way will ensure that each of you meets your daily average requirements for all these nutrients.

It encourages you to eat at least 'five a day'

As most of us are now aware, we should eat at least five portions of fruit and vegetables a day for good health. A diet high in fruit and vegetables has been linked with protection from all kinds of health problems including hypertension, heart disease, cancers, digestive problems, asthma, Syndrome X and obesity.

Fruits and vegetables are some of the best sources of vitamin C (an important immune system booster) as well as a range of other vitamins and minerals, including potassium.

Fruit and veg are linked to health not only because of the vitamins and minerals they contain, but also because of their content of phytochemicals – the plant chemicals that give the plants their colour, aroma and flavour. Most phytochemicals are powerful anti-oxidants, which help to prevent disease and, it is thought, may slow down the ageing process.

A diet high in fruit and veg provides soluble and insoluble fibre, important for a healthy digestive system and bowel movement – something that many people on restricted low-calorie diets often find a big problem. Foods high in soluble fibre also tend to contain pre-biotics, food components called oligosaccharides, which provide a source of food for healthy gut bacteria and allow them to thrive and can thus improve conditions such as Irritable Bowel Syndrome.

Lastly, a diet high in fresh fruit and vegetables is self-restricting in calorie content. Most of them are low or fairly low in calories and therefore if you eat them instead of, say, crisps or ice cream, you may lose weight, or maintain a healthy weight, more easily without having to restrict the actual amount of food that you eat.

The Traffic Light Diet encourages you to eat *at least* five portions of fruit and vegetables a day. Indeed, most of you following the diet will be eating more than that. All fresh fruits and vegetables apart from potatoes* (which are AMBER) are 'GREEN for Go' foods.

---

* Potatoes aren't classed as a 'five-a-day' vegetable by the UK government but are grouped with other starchy foods such as bread and rice.

It helps you reach and maintain a suitable weight in a healthy way

Obviously the main objective of the Traffic Light Diet is to help you to lose weight and keep the weight off. This in itself should help you to better health in the long term, as over-weight and obesity are linked with a long list of problems including heart disease and stroke, Type 2 diabetes, high blood pressure, some cancers including breast cancer and prostate cancer, insulin resistance, low back pain, arthritis, gout, polycystic ovary syndrome, depression and poor body image.

While some other diets may help you to shed weight easily, few can manage to help you maintain the weight loss over time. Research indicates that over 90 per cent of people who lose weight put it back on again, and either get stuck at a new, higher weight, or begin a period – some-times a lifetime – of 'yo-yo' dieting.

This 'yo-yo' syndrome – repeatedly losing and then putting on weight – most often occurs when people try to follow a diet that is too low in calories (a 'crash' diet). Crash diets encourage faddy eating and a poor control of eating habits. Crash dieting and 'yo-yo' dieting over a long period of time are both linked with health problems, including loss of lean tissue (muscle) and possible damage to internal organs. And, because constant yo-yo dieting increases the proportion of fat tissue to lean tissue (muscle) in the body, people who do this find it harder and harder to lose weight over time. This is because the decrease in lean tissue causes the metabolic rate to slow down, as muscle is more metabolically active than fat tissue.

Research shows that the best and most healthy way to lose weight and *keep it off* is on a diet that:

➡ helps you shed weight slowly

➡ helps you to create a daily calorie deficit of no more than about 500 a day (i.e. consume 500 calories fewer than your body is using)

➡ contains fat, protein and carbohydrates in sensible proportions (around 55–60 per cent carbohydrate, 15 per cent protein and 25–30 per cent fat)

➡ has principles that can be followed for a lifetime rather than just the duration of 'the diet'

The Traffic Light Diet fulfils all these criteria.

The Traffic Light Diet is constructed in such a way that you can follow its principles to carry on eating sensibly *for life*. For advice on whether or not you really do need to lose weight, see page 72, and for tips on following the plan after you reach your target weight, see below and on page 62.

Any weight-reducing or weight-maintenance diet needs to be accompanied by regular activity (see Chapter 7). Research shows that a combination of diet and exercise is the most successful way to stay slim in the long term.

Traffic Light – Now and for Life

This is a plan that you can use not only to lose weight but also to maintain weight. With minor adjustments, the Traffic Light Diet can be used for the rest of your life, not only to stay slim but also as a blueprint for healthy eating.

Let's first look at how you lose weight.

We all eat a certain number of calories each day. If you are overweight, you have probably been eating a few more calories on a daily basis than your body needs to produce the energy for living, activity and general body repair and maintenance. Those extra calories have nowhere to go and nothing to do, so your body cleverly converts them into fat and stores them in the fat cells all over the body.

In order to remove that stored fat, you need to get your body to convert it back into energy. This you can only do by reducing your calorie intake (or burning up lots more energy than normal in extra activity) so that your body no longer gets all the calories it needs from the food and drink that it takes in. At that point, it will start converting its fat supplies back into usable fuel and, hey presto, you begin to lose weight.

A clever dieter will eat and drink the right amount of calories in the day to produce a moderate calorie deficit so that weight is lost gradually (say, one pound a week, or two pounds a week at most). If you lose more than that, problems are likely to occur such as hunger pangs, feelings of dizziness and deprivation, and the diet is likely to be abandoned (don't we know it!).

Research shows that people who consume around 500 calories a day *less* than they use up in energy will be most successful in losing weight and keeping it off long term.

Five hundred calories a day isn't a great deal. To cut that amount of calories from your own diet, you might, for instance, replace a large glass of orange juice at breakfast with a kiwifruit (100 calories saved), swop a chocolate bar midmorning for an apple (250 calories saved), and drink two spritzers in the evening rather than two glasses of ordinary wine (150 calories saved). That's just a very broad and simple example of how following the Traffic Light Diet can save you the right amount of calories a day, and produce gradual, permanent weight loss.

(By the way, although the Traffic Light Diet doesn't ask you to actually count calories, it *does* work by reducing your calorie intake. This is how any successful slimming diet works, not by some 'magic' formula, no matter what anyone may tell you.)

Many diets ask you to reduce your daily calorie intake to 1,000 a day or less – and when you consider that many overweight people may have gained weight by consuming a total of 3,000 or 4,000 calories a day, that is a huge reduction. Rapid weight loss will result — and rapid return of weight once 'the diet' is over or, more likely, rapid abandonment of the diet after a few days of misery, to be followed by feelings of guilt and worthlessness.

On the Traffic Light Diet you get used to:

➔ **slightly smaller portions of certain foods**
➔ **slightly larger portions of other foods**
➔ **swopping a high-calorie food for a lower-calorie food**
➔ **having certain foods in very small, or very occasional, amounts**

This way you shed weight slowly and comfortably. Once you reach the weight that is right for you (which should not be too low), you can continue to eat in the Traffic Light way, but you're not left high and dry, as with so many diets.

💡 *You don't need to 'diet' for the rest of your life in order to keep the weight off!*

When I say that you can continue on the Traffic Light plan for the rest of your life in order to maintain your new slimmer body, I don't mean to imply that you must spend the rest of your days eating 'slimmer's' portions.

To shed those stones or, latterly, pounds, you will have been eating around 500 calories a day less than your body needs. Once you reach your target weight, you need to stop creating a calorie deficit, and start eating the right amount for your new, slim body's needs.

All you do is:

➔ **increase your intake of AMBER foods by around 30 per cent (by a combination of eating them more frequently and increasing portion sizes)**

→ **continue eating your fill of GREEN foods**
→ **continue to be wary of eating too many RED foods**

The principles are the same:

GREEN for go
AMBER – go carefully
RED – stop and think!

By increasing your AMBER portions, however, you will increase your regular calorie intake to a level that will help you to maintain your weight.

From time to time you will also be able to eat slightly larger amounts of some of the RED foods (e.g. an extra glass of wine, or an extra chocolate or two) and still not put on any weight. That is fine! All I will say is that, over time, your tastebuds do alter on the Traffic Light plan, and you may find that your taste for many of the RED foods has all but gone. In that case, don't encourage it back – but eat your fill of GREEN and AMBER foods instead.

As soon as you feel your waistband beginning to expand even a tiny tad, take it as a sign that your calorie intake is once more beginning to get a little too high, and go back to the original Traffic Light plan until that bloated feeling retreats. Some of you may prefer to take more regular exercise instead to burn off those surplus calories. I can't stress strongly enough that regular exercisers are the most successful at staying slim after a diet. The activity programmes in Chapter 7 are suitable for weight maintenance as well as weight reduction.

That, in essence, is all you need to do to follow the Traffic Light Maintenance Plan.

For a little more guidance on eating once the weight loss part of the plan is over, see page 62.

Traffic Light for Kids

There are not many adult dieting plans that are totally suitable for all the family, children over five included, and which are suitable whether family members need to lose weight or not.

The Traffic Light Diet is one of the few exceptions – so if, for example, you have bought this book wanting to shed some weight yourself, but the rest of your family has no need to, you will not have to prepare one meal for them and another for yourself. You all eat the same!

This diet is suitable for all because you simply adjust portion sizes of the AMBER foods so that people who don't need to lose weight get more calories.

Let me give you an example. You are having the Cod with Chilli Tomato Sauce for your evening meal (see recipe page 146). Non-slimming adult members of the family can have an extra one or more slices of wholemeal bread to add calories, or extra pasta, or an AMBER pudding (such as Greek yoghurt and fresh fruit). Children who are overweight between five and ten or eleven will probably do well on the standard Traffic Light Diet as their calorie needs are often broadly similar to an adult female's needs. Older children and teens need more calories so, again, portion sizes need to be increased accordingly.

Some parents say to me that their children don't like fruit and vegetables and will only eat items such as burgers and ice cream. The truth (which I discovered when researching the *Children's Food Bible* last year) is that experts know that if you get your children eating healthy foods before the age of two, those are the tastes that will tend to stick with them for life.

Small children can be faddy about food around the age of

two or three, but, in general, healthy children who get enough exercise will look forward to their healthy meals and snacks as much, if not more than, they would look forward to a less healthy diet based on saturated fats, sugar and salt.

So it is down to you, the parent/s, to be strong enough to avoid offering between-meal snacks of sweets, ice cream, biscuits, crisps and so on, and ensure your child is hungry for proper meals of real, good food, and to offer that real, good food instead of fast food and junk food.

I hope that the recipe suggestions within this book, and the wide choice of foodstuffs that are recommended on the Traffic Light Diet, will ensure that even though no child will like *every* food and drink, there is enough for even the faddiest child to choose from – with your guidance and encouragement.

I feel that it is vitally important to try to do just this – to help our children enjoy good food and not 'junk'. The *Obesity* report recognises that if we are, as a nation, to conquer the growing obesity problem in the West, then we need to make sure that our children start off right, eating a healthy diet from the moment they are weaned, and we need to make sure they don't put on too much weight during childhood.

I say the diet is suitable for children over five only because children younger than that may have special dietary needs. For example:

→ they should not be given whole nuts and seeds (which can cause choking, and allergic reactions to these foods are more common in children under five)
→ they may not be able to eat more than small amounts of fresh fruit and vegetables (their small digestive systems may not be able to cope)
→ because of their lower body weight, it may be wise for them

to have smaller amounts of some items like oily fish than older children and adults. (For more information on fish intake see the Chapter 4, Q22.)

For more information on pre-school childhood nutrition, go to the Food Standards Agency website (www.fsa.gov.uk)

However, most of the general principles of the Traffic Light Diet can be taken on board by any sensible parent for their small children – particularly the avoidance, most of the time, of the foods in the 'RED – Stop and Think' category. No child, no matter what their age, needs a diet that contains brightly coloured fizzy drinks, sweets that contain sugar, additives and little else, snack foods that contain nearly a whole day's sodium intake in one bag – and so on.

I stress that once children begin to be weaned, it is never too early to help them develop a taste for wholesome, nutritious foods rather than junk, convenience foods and snacks. Families who eat together tend to eat better food than those who don't – and, incidentally, tend to be happier families.

The next chapter will explain the simple basis for the Traffic Light Diet and will also provide you with sample menus for differing needs.

THE TRAFFIC LIGHT SYSTEM

In this chapter you will find everything you need to follow the entry-level Traffic Light Diet.

The diet itself is very simple because all foods come into one of three categories. These, with their subdivisions of food types, appear on pages 166–224. At the most basic level you can simply read these pages to follow the diet, choosing your own meals and snacks by mixing and matching the foods in the different colours according to these easy guidelines:

→ **eat all you like of the GREEN foods**
→ **eat moderate amounts of the AMBER foods**
→ **stop and think – eat only very occasionally, or in very small amounts, the RED foods**

This is all you need to know to begin *now*.

The pages containing this list appear again at the end of the book (pages 285–296) so that if necessary you can cut them out and keep them with you to refer to in the early days, when shopping or out and about.

For those of you who would like more help, in the form of diet plans that you can follow to lose weight, the last half of this chapter contains different sample plans for a single person, a family and a couple. You still don't have to count calories or weigh and measure food while following these plans. They simply show you how you can use the GREEN, AMBER and RED foods to build up a healthy diet and also illustrate how some of the Recipes (pages 112–165) can be used within your diet. If you like, you can simply use these pages to provide inspiration on different types of meals you can serve, from breakfasts through to quick lunches or suppers, or more leisurely main meals.

I think you will be pleasantly surprised at the variety of foods you can eat while losing weight the Traffic Light way.

A fourth sample week of menus, the Maintenance Diet, shows how easy it is to maintain your new slim weight following the Traffic Light system.

If you want more information about certain foods, turn to Chapter 6. You will find lists of all the major foods in chart form, so that you can:

→ **see at a glance what category each food is**
→ **read any special notes about that food, including recommended portion sizes**
→ **find any other notes of interest**

Chapter 4, 'Your Questions Answered', is devoted to answering all your questions about the Traffic Light Diet, healthy eating and slimming in general.

Do read through the whole of pages 44–5 before starting the diet and choosing which of the slimming diet plans you might like to try. Whilst there are few instructions to follow, there *is* some information that you need to take on board before beginning.

GREEN for Go Foods

These are the foods that you can 'eat as much as you like'.
What does this mean in practice?

→ **You should aim to add to each meal (in volume terms) as many items as you like from this list.**

→ You should have at least two items from this list on your plate at each meal.

→ You do not have to stint on portion sizes of these foods.

→ You should vary the items you choose from this list so that you don't get a surfeit of just one or two.

Even healthy, low-calorie options may sometimes be 'bad for you' at 'overdose' levels. For more information on this, see Chapter 4, Question 21.

→ You can choose items from this section for snacks when you feel hungry.

→ Choosing plenty of foods from this list should mean that you easily meet the Department of Health's advice for 'five a day' of fruit and vegetables. You should, however, aim to have at least half of your daily fruit and veg intake as vegetables.

→ Remember that you can mix any GREEN item with the correct amount of an AMBER item to make a 'new' food. For example, you might mix chickpeas with a moderate portion of olive oil (and seasonings) to produce Hummus (see the recipe for this on page 121).

→ You should aim for most vegetables and fruits to be fresh if possible, but frozen is fine. Canned in water (not brine or syrup) is also OK now and then, although the vitamin content tends to be diminished when items are canned. Dried fruits are listed under AMBER.

→ If choosing fish as a GREEN food, choose only those listed. For more information on eating fish, see Chapter 4, Question 22.

Vegetables

Artichoke, globe (fresh or canned in water); artichoke, Jerusalem; asparagus; aubergine.

Bamboo shoots; beans, broad; beans, French; beans, green; beans, runner; beansprouts; beetroot; broccoli, all types; Brussels sprouts.

Cabbage, red, white and green; cabbage, savoy; carrots; cauliflower; celeriac; celery; Chinese leaves; chicory; corn on the cob; courgettes; cucumber.

Endive; fennel; garlic; kale; leeks; lettuce, all kinds; mangetout peas; marrow; mushrooms; mustard and cress; okra; olives (fresh).

Onions, all kinds, including pickled; parsnips; peas; peppers, all colours; pumpkin; radish; rocket.

Salsify; seakale; spinach; spring greens; squash, all kinds; sugar snap peas; swede; sweetcorn kernels.

Tomatoes (fresh and canned); turnips; watercress.

Home-made vegetable soups (see recipes); home-made vegetable sauces (see recipes); commercial vegetable salsas.

Fruits

Apples, dessert or cooking; apricots; bananas, small; black-berries; blackcurrants; blueberries; cranberries; cherries; damsons; dates (fresh); figs (fresh); gooseberries; grape-fruit; grapes; greengages.

Kiwifruit; kumquats; lemons; limes; loganberries; lychees; mandarins; mangoes; medlars; melon, all kinds; nectarines; oranges.

Papaya (pawpaw); passion fruit; peaches; pears; pine-apples; plums; quinces; raspberries; satsumas; star fruit; strawberries; tangerines.

Herbs and spices

All fresh, dried or frozen herbs and spices, including chillies, garlic, ginger, basil, coriander, parsley, etc.

Dairy produce

Skimmed milk; o per cent fat natural fromage frais; natural low-fat bio yoghurt; soya milk and yoghurt.

Fish and seafood

All the following white (non-oily) fish:
Cod, haddock, plaice, skate, halibut, hake, turbot, monkfish, sole; tuna canned in water (a maximum of four cans a week for women who are pregnant or intending to become pregnant; see Chapter 4, Question 22), whiting, sea bass, red snapper, hake, mullet, sea bream.

SEAFOOD:

Crab, mussels, oysters, scallops (fresh or frozen).

Pulses and vegetarian proteins

Unsweetened calcium-enriched soya milk; low-fat, low-sugar soya yoghurt; all dried pulses (cooked according to packet instructions) or pulses canned in water, including red, brown and green lentils, chickpeas, red kidney beans, soya beans, butter-beans, cannellini beans, black-eye beans; haricot beans and split peas; Quorn, including pieces, chunks and fillets; tofu, silken or firm, natural; soya mince; home-made pulse soups (see recipes).

Grains

Wheatgerm.

Condiments

Vinegar (all kinds); lemon juice; piccallili; pickled beetroot.

Miscellaneous

Tomato purée, passata, sun-dried tomatoes, sun-blush tomatoes.

Drinks

Water; red-bush tea, camomile tea, peppermint tea, lemon balm tea, and other natural unsweetened herbal teas; tomato juice; vegetable juice.

AMBER – Go Carefully Foods

These are the foods that you can eat in moderate amounts.

In practice, if you are a female who wants to lose weight, this will usually mean choosing from the AMBER list:

→ *one* item at breakfast
→ *one* or *two* items at lunch
→ *two* or *three* items for your main meal

You should give yourself a small to medium portion for each item. You can also have a daily snack from the AMBER category, but try to ensure that, unless you have more than three stones to lose, your daily total of AMBER foods doesn't exceed *six*. (This excludes the AMBER drinks, advice on which appears in Chapter 4, Question 8, and the AMBER condiments, advice on which appears in Chapter 4, Question 9.)

The diet plans that follow show how you can use the AMBER foods within your particular diet. Remember – 'go carefully' doesn't mean 'avoid'! Just because a food is not particularly low in calories, it isn't necessarily 'bad'. In fact, it can often be very good for you. The AMBER group contains some of the healthiest foods you can eat, so you should choose from this section regularly. Items that are high (or highish) in calories (such as olive oil, nuts, seeds, avocados, whole grains and oily fish) all contain important nutrients so don't feel guilty for eating them. (Indeed, some of the foods in the AMBER group actually contain more calories than some in the RED group.)

Most of the 'unadulterated' animal protein foods (such as lean red meat and poultry) are in this group, as are most of the starchy carbohydrates such as potatoes and bread. These foods help to make up a balanced diet and while not all of them are particularly low in calories, in the main they are not particularly high either. They provide you not only with calories and/or proteins and starches, but also with various vitamins and minerals. Carbs provide fibre too.

For more detailed information on the nutritional benefits of particular foods and on my guidelines on portion size, see Chapter 6. See also Questions 24, 25 and 29 in Chapter 4 for advice on amounts of AMBER foods for different groups of people, such as non-dieters and males.

Vegetables

Potatoes of all types (e.g. new, old, salad varieties), boiled or baked; sweet potatoes; yams; avocados, guacamole; olives in oil; corn canned in brine; commercial vegetable soups from the chilled counter with no added cream; all ready-made, chilled-counter vegetable sauces for pasta or cooking containing no more than 60 calories per 100ml (check the label).

Fruit

Dried fruits, including dried apricots, peaches, prunes, apples, pears, figs, dates, raisins, sultanas, currants and cranberries; rhubarb.

Dairy produce and eggs

Semi-skimmed milk; goat's milk; natural whole milk bio yoghurt; natural Greek yoghurt or half-fat Greek style yoghurt; 8 per cent fat natural fromage frais; cottage cheese; feta cheese; fresh goat's cheese; Italian mozzarella cheese; half-fat Cheddar cheese; Brie; Camembert; reduced-fat cheese sauces and dips.

Hen's eggs (boiled or poached), duck eggs, quail's eggs.

Fish and shellfish

Swordfish,* shark,* marlin,* and all the following oily fish, fresh or frozen:

Salmon, tuna, mackerel, trout, sardines, pilchards, sprats, herring, kipper, eel, jellied eel, carp.

Mackerel, pilchards or sardines canned in tomato sauce.

SEAFOOD:

Lobster, prawns, squid, octopus.

---

* Women who are pregnant or intending to become pregnant, and children under sixteen should avoid these fish. See Chapter 4, Question 22, for more specific advice on oily and other fish consumption for different groups.

Meat, poultry, game

Beef – all lean cuts, including extra-lean minced beef, steak (remove fat band), lean roast beef; leg of lamb (skin removed); lamb steaks and fillet; pork fillet (tenderloin); pork steaks; leg of pork (excluding fat and skin); lean ham (reduced-salt varieties).

Chicken, all cuts (skin removed before eating); turkey, all cuts and mince; pheasant; duck meat (excluding fat and skin); guinea fowl, venison, veal, rabbit, pigeon and any other game birds; kidneys and liver (avoid if pregnant).

Offal, including liver and kidneys.

Pulses and vegetarian proteins

Baked beans in tomato sauce; ready-made hummus; TVP (textured vegetable protein) mince; soya mince; ready-made lentil pâté; ready-made mushroom pâté; ready-made hazelnut pâté; ready-made felafel patties; ready-made bean burgers; ready-made pulse soups; refried beans.

Nuts and seeds

All fresh nuts, including almonds, chestnuts, peanuts, macadamias, walnuts, brazils, hazelnuts, cashews, pecans (excluding coconut); ready-made nut roast.

All fresh seeds, including pine kernels, sunflower seeds, poppy seeds, pumpkin seeds, flaxseeds.

Grains, baked goods and cereals

Basmati brown rice, basmati white rice; bulghur wheat; rolled oats; pot barley; quinoa; traditional couscous.

Wholewheat pasta and noodles; wholewheat/wholemeal

bread; oatbread; granary bread; dark rye bread; brown bread; white bread; wholewheat pitta bread, white pitta bread; chapati; flatbread.

Ready-made, shop-bought, vegetable- or fish-topped thin and crispy pizza, or home-made pizza (see recipes).

Oatcakes with no added sugar; brown rice cakes; dark rye crispbreads.

BREAKFAST CEREALS:

No added-sugar muesli; porridge, instant oat cereal; wholewheat breakfast biscuits; Shredded Wheat; Puffed Wheat; All Bran, Bran Flakes; Cheerios; Fruit 'n' Fibre.

Fats and oils

Groundnut (peanut) oil, olive oil, sesame seed oil, walnut oil, rapeseed oil, cooking oil spray; traditional French dressing.

Miscellaneous

All shop-bought, ready-made main meals containing less than 10g fat per portion (check the label); all takeaway main meals containing less than 20g fat and 500 calories per portion.

Ready-made sandwiches containing less than 10g fat and 300 calories per portion; ready salads containing no more than 10g fat and 300 calories per portion.

Skimmed or semi-skimmed coconut milk.

Condiments

Low-salt stock cubes or bouillon; low- and reduced-fat salad dressings and sauces, including reduced-fat salad cream and mayonnaise; chutney and pickles; fruit relishes; mustard; tomato ketchup.

> **Note**: See Chapter 4, Question 9, for more information about the use of condiments.

Snacks

Pretzels.

Drinks

Coffee; green tea, white tea, black tea, oolong tea; pure fruit smoothies made with whole fruit at home (see recipes); soda water.

> **Note**: See Chapter 4, Question 8, for more information about drinking coffee and tea.

RED – Stop and Think Foods

These are the foods that you should eat either only occasionally, or in very small amounts, or not at all. While you are trying to lose weight, your should aim for a daily maximum of no more than two small portions of RED foods.

Most RED foods are very high in calories. Often high-calorie foods also tend to be less good for us for other reasons (e.g. they are high in saturated fat and/or salt and/or sugar and/or various additives – or, perhaps, they are just very low in nutrients in comparison with their calorie content). Sometimes they are not particularly bad for us, but are just very high in calories and need to be limited in order to help weight loss.

Because this is a healthy diet as well as a slimming diet, some of the foods in this group are not high in calories but, for various reasons, have been included here – for instance, 'diet' soft drinks.

Where an exclamation mark (!) appears next to a food, it indicates one of the few foods that I recommend you avoid altogether, for reasons explained in Chapter 4, Questions 17 and 18.

If a food or drink doesn't appear on the GREEN or AMBER lists, then assume that it is a RED food.

For more advice on RED foods, see Chapter 4, Question 13. Chapter 6 offers detailed information on RED foods, including portion sizes, specific qualities, etc. Also the diet plans at the end of this chapter have incorporated RED foods into the various week's menus.

Vegetables

Chips, fried; chips, oven; chips, microwave; potato salad; olives in brine; breaded onion rings; breaded mushrooms; vegetable crispbakes; cream of vegetable soups.

Fruit

Dried banana chips; olives in brine.

Nuts and seeds

Salted nuts of any kind, e.g. salted cashews or peanuts; roasted seeds (salted or otherwise); coconut; coconut cream, full-fat coconut milk, tahini.

Dairy produce

Cream, all kinds, including half-fat; Greek yoghurt, full-fat; fruit-flavoured yoghurts (low-fat, low-calorie or full-fat, high-calorie); fruit-flavoured fromage frais; full-fat milk; goat's milk.

Eggs, any kind, fried.

CHEESES:

Cheddar; cream cheese; mascarpone; Danish Blue; Edam; Gruyère; Parmesan; processed cheese slices; Stilton and all full-fat/hard/blue cheeses; full-fat cheese sauces and dips; blue cheese dressing.

Fish and shellfish

Battered fish of any kind; deep-fried fish of any kind; tara-masalata; fish canned in oil, fish canned in brine; smoked salmon and other smoked fish, e.g. kippers.

Meat, poultry

All fatty cuts of meat, e.g. shoulder of lamb; lamb chops; pork crackling; pork spare ribs; pork chops including fat; poultry with the skin left on; beefsteak with the fat band left on; all minced beef and burgers unless labelled extra-lean; duck including fat; goose.

Sausages, all; black pudding; delicatessen cuts, including salami, chorizo, kabana, mortadella, pepperoni; bacon, all types, including ham (unless reduced-salt); scotch eggs.

Meat pâtés, all; corned beef; meat pies and pasties with pastry; ready-made, shop-bought, meat-topped pizzas.

Grains, baked goods and cereals

Any rice excluding basmati; pearl barley; white pasta; white noodles; instant couscous; polenta; pearl barley.

White rice cakes; wheat crackers of all kinds, e.g. cream crackers, water biscuits, all biscuits for cheese; cheese straws.

Flour.

Sweet biscuits, sweet snack bars, cereal bars and cookies of all kinds.

All cakes; commercial fruit pies and tarts.

All commercial savoury pies, quiches, tarts.

French bread; garlic bread; naan bread; croissants, scones, teacakes and similar.

All cereals with added sugars/honey, including corn-flakes, Frosties, Coco Pops, crunch-type baked cereal mix; chocolate-coated cereals; cereals with added chocolate/caramel.

Snacks

Potato crisps or similar potato snacks (all); all savoury snack packets except pretzels e.g. Bombay mix, tortilla chips, oriental mix; popcorn; Twiglets.

Fats and oils

Butter, margarine, blended vegetable oils, corn oil, sunflower oil, safflower oil, dripping, lard, suet, low-fat spread.

Confectionery

All chocolate; all sweets (!); sugar; honey.

Desserts and ices

All commercial desserts and ices, including custards, mousses, instant packet desserts; jellies; flans, cheesecakes, sponges, trifle, caramel desserts, rice pudding, meringues, roulade, chocolate puddings, eclairs; ice cream tubs; individual ice creams and lollies.

Condiments

Mayonnaise, full-fat; full-fat dressings; hollandaise sauce; peanut butter, jams; salt; soya sauce; processed meals and snacks containing more than 1.25g salt (0.5g sodium) per 100g.

Miscellaneous

All ready-made, pour-over or cook-in sauces (for pasta, meat, etc.) containing more than 60 calories per 100g (check the label); all takeaway meals e.g. Chinese, Thai, Indian, Greek, burger bar, fish and chips; pizza, deep-pan, cheese or meat; all shop-bought ready main meals containing more than 20g fat per portion (check the label).

All shop-bought ready salads, sandwiches or light meals containing more than 300 calories per portion and/or more than 10g fat per portion (check the label).

Tinned soup, packet dried soup.

Drinks

All carbonated (fizzy) soft drinks both 'diet' and original (!); all squashes and cordials (!); all ready-made 'juice drinks' (!); all fruit juices; all alcoholic drinks; all traditional and instant-type hot milk drinks, e.g. chocolate, malt; all commercial flavoured waters, both 'diet' and non-diet versions.

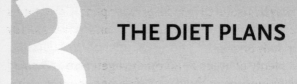

THE DIET PLANS

It is easy to devise your own daily diet using the GREEN, AMBER and RED lists on pages 30–43. If you would prefer to use a ready-made plan, however, the following three all provide you with a daily menu of balanced eating. First decide which is most appropriate for you – the singles' diet, the family diet or the couples' diet. Lastly, there is a weight maintenance plan. Even if you don't follow a plan, it may be a useful blueprint to see how the Traffic Light system works in practice.

As you will see, there really is no weighing or measuring involved, unless you are following some of the recipes. If you are a female dieter, simply take note of the guidance on portion sizes where given, and also be guided by your own appetite and needs.

In general, those with more than three stone to lose, non-dieters, men and teenagers will have larger portions of the AMBER foods – and perhaps extra portions – than dieting women who do not have a lot of weight to lose, and children under twelve. For further advice on this, see Chapter 4, Questions 7, 24, 25 and 29.

GREEN items

Don't forget that although foods from the GREEN list appear in the diets throughout, because they are to be added freely to the diet, you can eat them as much as you like. This may be useful to help fill up your plate, or for times when you feel hungry between meals and have already eaten your daily Snack.

Do add plenty of greens and other vegetables and salad items to your lunches and main meals when you can.

Drinks

Every day have plenty to drink (1.5 litres minimum). Choose most of your fluid from the GREEN drinks and a moderate amount, if you like, from the AMBER drinks. Further notes on drinks appear in Chapter 4, Question 8, and in the Food Reference Charts.

Snacks

The items listed under Snacks are healthy items that you can add to your daily diet, to be eaten at a time of day when you often feel hungry. For many people, this is around 4 or 5 p.m., to help you through the gap between lunch and your main meal.

RED foods

The items listed under RED Extras (which don't appear every day) are RED items that, as we've seen, you can choose occasionally and/or in very small amounts. There will also be small amounts of RED items used within the meal plans – for example, butter, honey or hard cheeses. Use these diet plans as an instant reference for a healthy level of RED items.

Singles' Plan

Don't forget that where any portion guidelines are given, they are for female dieters with under three stones to lose. Other dieters and non-dieters, especially teens, will need larger portions; see Chapter 4, Questions 7, 24 and 25.

Don't forget to add your drinks (see previous page).

....

DAY ONE

Breakfast
– 1 large bowl low-fat natural bio yoghurt
– 1 chopped orange
– grapes
– 1 dessertspoonful sunflower seeds
– 1–2 teaspoons runny honey

Lunch
– 1 medium portion low-salt, low-sugar baked beans in tomato sauce
– 1 medium slice wholemeal toast with a little low-fat spread

Main meal
– 1 portion red mullet, tilapia or sea bass, cleaned and grilled, baked or steamed with chopped chilli, garlic, ginger, black pepper and a dash of olive oil until cooked
– large selection of fresh vegetables (e.g. green beans, baby corn cobs, sliced carrot, broccoli), stir-fried in a dash of olive oil
– 1 apple

Snack
– 1 small banana

RED Extras
– 2 dark chocolates

....

DAY TWO

Breakfast
– 1 medium bowl muesli (no added sugar or salt variety, high in nuts and seeds)
– 1 chopped apple
– skimmed milk

Lunch
– 1 portion yellowfin tuna canned in water, drained and mixed with a medium portion of cooked wholewheat pasta shapes, chopped tomato, cucumber and red pepper, all tossed in a dressing made from 1 level tablespoon reduced-fat mayonnaise mixed with low-fat bio yoghurt and lemon juice
– 1 kiwifruit

Main meal
– 1 medium chicken breast, sliced and stir-fried in a non-stick pan with a dash of groundnut oil and a selection of stir-fried vegetables, e.g. mangetout, Chinese leaves, beansprouts and yellow pepper, with a dash of teriyaki sauce and a little low-salt chicken stock added towards the end of cooking time
– 1 medium portion brown basmati rice

Snack
– 1 handful mixed nuts and raisins

RED Extras
– Small portion Greek yoghurt with 1 teaspoon honey

....

DAY THREE

Breakfast
– 1 pack ready-made exotic fruit salad, topped with 1 small tub low-fat natural fromage frais, 1 teaspoon of runny honey and a sprinkling of flaxseeds

Lunch
– 1 ready-made ham and salad sandwich on wholemeal bread no more than 300 calories (check label)
– 1 apple
– grapes

Main meal
– 1 portion Quick Spicy Lentil Soup (see recipe page 113)
– large mixed salad with olive oil vinaigrette
– 1 medium slice pumpernickel bread

Snack
– 1 handful dried ready-to-eat apricots

RED Extra
– 1 glass white wine

....

DAY FOUR
Breakfast
– As Day One

Lunch
– 1 portion Hummus (see recipe page 121)
– 1 wholemeal pitta
– 1 apple
– 1 pear

Main meal
– 1 medium portion pork tenderloin, cut into bite-sized cubes and threaded on to a kebab stick with diced red pepper and red onion, brushed with olive oil and grilled until cooked through
– 1 small to medium portion brown basmati rice
– large green side salad with oil-free French dressing

Snack
– 1 handful fresh nuts, e.g. almonds

....

DAY FIVE

Breakfast
– As Day Two

Lunch
– 1 medium portion Brie
– 3 oatcakes
– tomatoes
– spring onions
– watercress
– 1 orange

Main meal
– 1 medium salmon steak served with a little good-quality ready-made green pesto sauce
– 1 medium portion wholewheat pasta shapes
– broccoli
– peas

Snack
– 1 handful sunflower or pumpkin seeds

RED Extra
– 1 glass white wine

....

DAY SIX

Breakfast
– As Day Three

Lunch
– 1 small avocado, sliced and combined with sliced tomato, rocket and 1 tablespoon pine nuts in olive oil vinaigrette
– 2 brown rice cakes

Main meal
– 1 individual Mediterranean Vegetable Pizza (see recipe page 148)
– large green salad of various coloured salad leaves with oil-free French dressing

Snack
– 1 small banana

RED Extra
– 2 dark chocolates

....

DAY SEVEN

Breakfast
– 1 boiled egg
– 1 slice wholemeal bread with low-fat spread
– 1 orange
– 1 kiwifruit

Lunch
– 1 portion Quick Spicy Lentil Soup (see recipe page 113)
– 1 slice pumpernickel bread
– 1 apple

Main meal
– 1 small to medium lamb steak, grilled
– large mixed salad with oil-free French dressing *or* a selection of vegetables to include spinach or cabbage plus carrots
– 1 small to medium portion new potatoes

Snack
– 1 portion low-fat natural bio yoghurt

RED extras
– 1 glass red wine *or* 1 individual tub ready-made fruit mousse

Family Plan

Note: Children following this plan should have 0.5 litre skimmed or semi-skimmed milk in addition to the meals listed and the other drinks recommended (see 'Drinks' p. 45), whether or not they are watching their weight.

Remember that any portion guidelines given are for female dieters with less than three stones to lose, and children aged between five and eleven who need to watch their weight. Non-dieters of all ages, and dieting teens and men, will need to alter portion sizes to suit themselves. These groups can also add extra portions of AMBER foods to their meals (e.g. a slice of bread at breakfast), and/or have large portions of AMBER foods rather than small or medium ones, and/or have one or two extra Snacks a day.

For detailed information on AMBER portions for various groups of people, see Chapter 4, Questions 7, 24, 25 and 29.

....

DAY ONE
Breakfast
– 2 Weetabix
– skimmed milk
– 1 pear

Lunch
– 1 portion Cheesy Coleslaw (see recipe page 124)
– 1 medium portion turkey breast slices
– large mixed salad with oil-free French dressing *or* low-calorie salad cream
– 2 oatcakes

Main meal
– 1 portion Beef and Tomato Casserole (see recipe page 131)
– 1 small to medium portion wholewheat noodles *or* brown basmati rice
– peas
– dark leafy greens, e.g. cabbage, kale, spinach

Snack
– 1 apple

RED Extras
– 1 individual chocolate mousse, no more than 120 calories per pot (check label)

....

DAY TWO
Breakfast
– 1 large bowl low-fat natural bio yoghurt with 1–2 teaspoons of runny honey

– 1 satsuma
– red grapes
– 1–2 teaspoons sunflower seeds or chopped nuts

Lunch
– 1 medium portion scrambled egg, made with skimmed milk and cooked in a little low-fat spread in a non-stick saucepan, with chopped tomato added towards end of cooking time
– 1 medium slice wholemeal toast
– 1 small handful dried ready-to-eat apricots

Main meal
– 1 portion Chunky Vegetable and Bean Soup (see recipe page 115)
– 1 medium slice wholemeal bread
– 1 portion Baked Bananas (see recipe page 159)

Snack
– 1 handful fresh nuts, e.g. hazelnuts

RED Extra
– 1 small slice good quality fruit cake

....

DAY THREE

Breakfast
– large bowl porridge made with half skimmed milk, half water
– 1–2 teaspoons runny honey
– 1 apple

Lunch
– 1 small to medium portion mackerel fillets in tomato sauce
– 1 medium slice wholemeal bread with low-fat spread
– cucumber

– watercress
– 1 pear

Main meal
– 1 medium baked potato
– 1 portion Chilli Con Carne (see recipe page 132)
– 1 portion Guacamole (see recipe page 122)
– large green salad, using leaves of different colours and oil-free French dressing

Snack
– 1 small banana

RED Extra
– 1 individual pot low-fat custard

....

DAY FOUR

Breakfast
– As Day One

Lunch
– 1 portion Red Lentil and Squash Soup (see recipe page 116)
– 1 medium portion dark rye bread
– 1 small portion Greek yoghurt (half-fat or full-fat) with 1 teaspoon runny honey

Main meal
– 1 portion Turkey Cheeseburger (see recipe page 135)
– large mixed salad with oil-free French dressing
– tomato ketchup

Snack
– 1 slice melon plus 4 stoned prunes *or* 2 dried figs

Red Extra
– 1 individual tub fruit-flavoured fromage frais

....

DAY FIVE

Breakfast

– As Day Two

Lunch
– 1 medium portion low-salt, low-sugar baked beans in tomato sauce
– 1 medium portion wholemeal toast with a little low-fat spread
– 1 satsuma

Main meal
– 1 portion Chicken and Prawn Sizzle (see recipe page 136)
– 1 medium portion brown basmati rice

Snack
– red grapes

RED Extra
– 1 individual chocolate-covered biscuit bar

....

DAY SIX

Breakfast
– As Day Three

Lunch
- 1 portion ready-made, chilled-counter carrot and coriander soup
- 1 small piece Brie or half-fat Cheddar *or* 1 medium portion soft goat's cheese
- 1 medium portion dark rye bread
- 1 apple

Main meal
- 1 medium portion roast pork leg
- 1 small to medium portion potatoes, brushed with groundnut oil and roasted
- 2 portions green vegetables of choice
- carrots
- 1–2 teaspoons apple sauce
- fat-skimmed gravy

Snack
- 1 small banana

RED Extra
- 1 small portion pork crackling *or* 1 small portion vanilla ice cream

....

DAY SEVEN

Breakfast
- 1 poached egg
- 1 portion sliced dark-gilled mushrooms or halved tomatoes, stir-fried in a little groundnut oil
- 1 medium portion wholemeal toast

Lunch
- 1 wholemeal pitta bread, filled with sliced extra-lean, reduced-

salt ham and a selection of chopped salad items plus oil-free
French dressing
– 1 satsuma

Main meal
– 1 portion Family Fish Pie (see recipe page 141)
– peas
– broccoli
– 1 apple

Snack
– 1 handful mixed nuts and raisins

Couples' Plan

As with the Family Plan, any portion guidelines given within
the meal and snack suggestions are for female dieters with
less than three stone to lose. Women with more than that to
lose, male slimmers and all non-dieters can have extra
Snacks or further additions of AMBER foods to the meals or
have larger portions.

For more information on AMBER foods for different
groups of people, see Chapter 4, Questions 7, 24, 25 and
28.

Don't forget your drinks (see the introduction to the Diet
Plans, page 44–5).

DAY ONE

Breakfast
– 1 portion Fruit and Yoghurt Smoothie (see recipe page 164)
– 1 handful walnuts

Lunch
– 1 open sandwich, made from 1 large slice wholemeal bread, with a little low-fat spread and plenty of mixed salad leaves, topped with plenty of dressed crab, black pepper, lemon juice and a little reduced-fat mayonnaise
– 1 apple
– red grapes

Main meal
– 1 portion Chilli Fried Chicken with Coriander (see recipe page 137) (Note: this dish can also be made with beef rather than chicken – see recipe tips)
– 1 small to medium portion wholewheat noodles
– broccoli florets garnished with sesame seeds

Snack
– 1 handful dried ready-to-eat apricots

RED Extra
– 1 glass white wine

....

DAY TWO

Breakfast
– 1 bowl muesli
– skimmed milk
– 1 small banana
– 1 orange

Lunch
– 1 portion Summer Vegetable Soup with Crudités (see recipe page 117)
– 1 medium slice wholemeal bread
– 1 small piece Brie or half-fat Cheddar cheese
– 1 pear

Main meal
– 1 portion Brochette of Monkfish and Prawns (see recipe page 143)
– 1 medium portion brown basmati rice
– large mixed salad with oil-free French dressing

Snack
– 4 brazil nuts

RED Extra
– 4 squares dark chocolate

....

DAY THREE

Breakfast
– 2 Shredded Wheat
– skimmed milk
– 1 apple
– 1 kiwifruit

Lunch
– 1 flatbread filled with plenty of canned tuna in water, well drained, plenty of chopped salad items (e.g. cucumber, onion, tomato, pepper) and a little reduced-fat mayonnaise mixed with 1 teaspoon of French mustard
– 1 small banana

Main meal
– 1 portion Mezze Platter (see recipe page 150)

Snack
– 1 handful stoned prunes *or* 2 dried ready-to-eat figs

RED Extra
– 1 glass white wine

....

DAY FOUR

Breakfast
– As Day One

Lunch
– 1 small portion Italian mozzarella, sliced and served with plenty of sliced tomato and basil and a little olive oil and lemon juice
– 1 small slice dark rye bread
– 1 apple

Main meal
– 1 portion Chicken, Aubergine and Garlic Roast (see recipe page 138)
– 1 small to medium portion new potatoes
– spinach

Snack
– 1 handful raisins

RED Extra
– 4 squares dark chocolate

....

DAY FIVE

Breakfast
– As Day Two

Lunch
– 1 portion Watermelon and Crisp Parma Ham Salad (see recipe page 125)

– 2 oatcakes
– 1 small banana

Main meal
– 1 portion Peppers Stuffed with Herb Rice (see recipe page 151)
– large mixed salad with oil-free French dressing
– 1 individual tub low-fat natural fromage frais with 2 teaspoons runny honey

Snack
– 1 small handful pumpkin seeds

....

DAY SIX

Breakfast
– As Day Three

Lunch
– 1 portion Cannellini Bean Dip (see recipe page 123)
– crudités
– 1 slice pumpernickel bread cut into strips
– 1 satsuma

Main meal
– 1 portion Greek Marinated Lamb (see recipe page 133)
– green beans
– 1 small to medium portion traditional couscous

Snack
– 1 small handful mixed nuts and raisins

RED Extra
– 1 glass red wine

....

DAY SEVEN

Breakfast
- 1 slice watermelon
- 1 portion low-fat natural fromage frais
- sprinkling of mixed fresh seeds
- 1 teaspoon runny honey

Lunch
- 1 large slice dark rye bread topped with low-fat spread, 1 hard-boiled egg, sliced, plenty of salad leaves, sliced tomato, cress and a drizzling of olive oil vinaigrette
- 1 small banana

Main meal
- 1 portion Trout Fillets with Almond Pesto (see recipe page 144)
- 1 small portion new potatoes
- broccoli
- peas

Snack
- 1 small handful stoned prunes *or* 2 ready-to-eat dried figs

RED extra
- 4 squares dark chocolate

Maintenance Plan and Tips

This maintenance plan can be used to maintain your new slim weight. Portions of AMBER food for women who have reached their target weight are increased to a maximum of **eight** a day.

Any portion guidelines given are for female non-dieters. Male non-dieters and teenagers may need larger portions –

or they can have extra Snacks or extra AMBER items.

For more information on numbers of portions for weight maintenance for different groups of people, see Chapter 4, Question 29.

Don't forget your drinks (see the introduction to the Diet Plans, page 44–5).

 Tips for maintaining your new slim self

• You don't have to stick to a very low calorie diet for the rest of your life in order to stay slim. Many people go wrong after they finish a slimming diet by returning to the way of eating that caused them to gain weight in the first place.

• If you stick to a healthy regime of the type of foods, like those that you have been eating on the Traffic Light Diet, you will be able to eat more, without putting on weight.

• Once you come off the Traffic Light Diet proper, this maintenance diet simply increases your ration of AMBER foods, while increasing portion sizes and slightly raising the amount of RED foods that you can eat.

• If you ever begin to gain weight again, you should immediately cut back slightly on your portions of AMBER foods and reduce the amount of RED foods that you eat.

Devising your own long-term eating plan

This book contains all the information you need about eating for slimness and good health for the rest of your life.

Once you have tried the maintenance plan below, you

can easily invent your own diet by following the basic Traffic Light Plan using the GREEN, AMBER and RED food groups on pages 29–43. You can add recipes from Chapter 5 or devise your own, using the Food Reference Charts in Chapter 6 for further detail on any particular food.

And, of course, it will help you stay slim in the future if you continue to exercise regularly.

For other information about weight maintenance, see Chapter 4, Question 29.

....

DAY ONE

Breakfast

– 3 medium tomatoes, halved and fried in a little groundnut oil in a non-stick pan, served on 1 large slice wholemeal toast with low-fat spread, topped with 1 tablespoon grated half-fat Cheddar cheese

Lunch

– 1 portion Salad Niçoise (see recipe page 126)
– 1 slice cantaloupe melon

Main meal

– 1 portion Caribbean Chicken with Rice and Peas (see recipe page 140)
– tomato and onion salad
– 1 portion Autumn Fruit Crumble (see recipe page 160)
– 1 small portion Greek yoghurt

Snack

– 1 brown rice cake with 1 tablespoon Hummus (see recipe page 121)

RED Extra
– 1 glass white wine

....

DAY TWO

Breakfast
– 1 large bowl porridge made with skimmed milk
– 2 teaspoons honey
– 1 pear, chopped
– sprinkling of flaxseeds and chopped nuts

Lunch
– 1 portion Vichyssoise soup (see recipe page 118)
– 1 medium slice wholemeal bread
– 1 tablespoon grated half-fat Cheddar cheese
– 1 apple

Main meal
– 1 portion Mushroom and Noodle Stir-fry (see recipe page 152)
– 1 portion Berry Compote Fool (see recipe page 161)

Snack
– 1 portion Fruit and Yoghurt Smoothie (see recipe page 164)

RED Extra
– 1 glass red wine

....

DAY THREE

Breakfast
– 1 medium bowl muesli
– skimmed milk
– 1 apple, chopped

– red grapes
– 1 small slice wholemeal bread with low-fat spread and low-sugar jam

Lunch
– 1 portion Red Pepper Soup (see recipe page 119)
– 1 medium slice dark rye bread
– 1 individual tub low-fat fromage frais
– 2 teaspoons runny honey
– red grapes

Main meal
– 1 portion Sweet Potato Balti (see recipe page 153)
– 1 medium portion brown basmati rice
– low-fat natural bio yoghurt with cucumber
– mango chutney

Snack
– 4 brazil nuts and 1 handful sultanas

RED Extra
– half a naan bread

....

DAY FOUR

Breakfast
– As Day Two

Lunch
– 1 portion Pesto Chicken Salad (see recipe page 127)
– 1 apple
– 1 orange

Main meal
– 1 medium portion wholewheat spaghetti
– 1 medium portion ready-made chilled-counter tomato sauce for pasta
– 2 tablespoons grated Parmesan cheese
– large green mixed-leaf salad with oil-free French dressing

Snack
– 1 small slice wholemeal bread with a little peanut butter (no added sugar variety)

RED Extra
– 1 small (30g) chocolate bar

....

DAY FIVE

Breakfast
– As Day Two

Lunch
– 1 large portion low-salt, low-sugar baked beans in tomato sauce
– 1 medium slice wholemeal toast with low-fat spread
– 1 orange

Main meal
1 portion Mediterranean Vegetable Pizza (see recipe page 148)
100g portion microwaveable chips
1 grilled tomato
peas

Snack
1 medium portion low-fat cheese dip, from the ready-made chilled counter
1 oatcake

RED Extra
– 1 glass white wine

....

DAY SIX

Breakfast
– As Day Three

Lunch
– 1 medium portion lentil or mushroom pâté, from the ready-made chilled counter
– 2 oatcakes
– large mixed salad with olive oil French dressing
– 1 slice cantaloupe melon

Main meal
– 1 medium portion lean roast beef
– 1 small portion potatoes, roasted in groundnut oil
– carrots
– spring greens
– fat-skimmed gravy
– horseradish sauce
– 1 portion Winter Fruit Salad (see recipe page 163)
– 1 small portion Greek yoghurt

Snack
– 1 small banana

....

DAY SEVEN

Breakfast
– 1 medium portion scrambled egg made with skimmed milk and a little knob of butter

– 1 medium slice wholemeal toast
– 1 orange *or* 2 satsumas

Lunch
– 1 medium portion Hummus (see recipe page 121)
– 2 dark rye crispbreads
– red pepper and onion salad with oil-free French dressing

Main meal
– 1 portion Cod with Chilli Tomato Sauce (see recipe page 146)
– 1 medium portion wholewheat pasta shapes
– broccoli

Snack
– 1 handful dried apricots
– 1 small slice wholemeal bread with a little peanut butter (no added sugar variety)

RED extra
– 1 glass red wine

YOUR QUESTIONS ANSWERED

This chapter answers your general questions on weight loss and gives more detailed advice on following the Traffic Light Diet. For your convenience, the questions that appear in this chapter are listed here in order with the page number on which they appear:

Questions

Q1 How do I know if I need to lose weight? See page 72

Q2 How does the Traffic Light Diet work to help me lose weight without calorie counting? See page 77

Q3 What do I do if my weight loss slows down or stops? See page 78

Q4 I have problems in my life that make dieting difficult – what advice do you have? See page 79

Q5 I want to follow the diet but my tastebuds are just so tuned to sugar and fat – not to mention salt! Any advice? See page 83

Q6 Dieting is boring – how do we get round that? See page 84

Q7 How many AMBER food portions can I eat a day while slimming? See page 84

Q8 What quantity of the AMBER drinks can I have? See page 86

Q9 What quantity of the AMBER condiments can I have? See page 87

Q10 What are the best choices from the AMBER carbohydrates? See page 89

Q11 How can I tell if a ready meal is RED or AMBER? See page 91

Q12 Would it be best to buy organic foods? See page 91

Q13 RED foods are allowed in small amounts but can you give me some further guidelines? See page 92

Q14 Is there a best way of incorporating the RED foods into my diet? See page 93

Q15 Why is there so little alcohol allowed on the diet? See page 94

Q16 What sort of chocolate do you recommend? See page 94

Q17 Why do you advise avoiding all sweets apart from chocolate? See page 95

Q18 Why do you suggest avoiding all fizzy drinks and squashes including those labelled 'low in calories'? See page 96

Q19 Why are fruit juices on your list of RED foods? See page 96

Q20 Can I add salt to my food? See page 97

Q21 Why are some of the GREEN foods bad for you in large quantities? See page 98

Q22 If fish is such a healthy food, why are many varieties not in the GREEN group? See page 99

Q23 How can I follow the Traffic Light system when eating out? See page 102

Q24 Do the menus and recipes listed contain enough calories for men or teens who need to lose weight? See page 104

Q25 What changes to the Traffic Light Diet plans do non-dieting members of the family have to make? See page 105

Q26 Why is the diet not suitable for children under five? See page 106

Q27 Is the diet suitable for diabetics and those with heart disease or cancer? See page 107

Q28 Is the diet suitable during pregnancy and breastfeeding? See page 107

Q29 What tips do you have for following the Traffic Light system for weight maintenance? See page 109

Question 1: How do I know if I need to lose weight?

There are several ways you can tell. Many people rely on the tried and tested simple ways – such as realising that none of your trousers or skirts fits you any more, or a look in the mirror that reveals a large pot belly or rolls of fat here and there.

Whilst these methods are generally reliable there is a slightly more scientific guide, which is hardly any more bother. It is called the Waist Circumference test (below), which I have adapted slightly.

Waist circumference test

All you do is grab yourself a tape measure and measure your waist! Then read off the results below.

MEN

Waist measurement 34 in or below: You are unlikely to be overweight unless you are much shorter than average. If you are still in doubt, do the BMI test (below).

Waist measurement 34.5–37 in: You are unlikely to have any health risks from being overweight. However, you may be a little overweight and should take care not to put on any more weight. Try the BMI test to confirm whether or not you should lose weight (see below). You may need to do more regular exercise to keep your waistline in trim.

Waist measurement 37–40 in: You are overweight and you have a slightly increased risk of health problems. You should lose weight.

Waist measurement over 40 in: You are significantly over-weight and you are at substantially increased risk of health problems. You should lose weight.

WOMEN

Waist measurement below 30 in: You are unlikely to be overweight unless you are much shorter than average. If you are still in doubt, do the BMI test (below).

Waist measurement 30–31.5 in: You may be a little overweight but this doesn't pose any health problems at the moment. Do the BMI test (see below) to confirm whether you are overweight. If you don't need to actively diet, you should watch your weight and perhaps take more exercise.

Waist measurement 31.5–34.5 in: You are overweight and have an increased risk of health problems. You should lose weight.

Waist measurement over 34.5 in: You are overweight and have a substantially increased risk of health problems. You should lose weight.

The reason why the waist measurement is important, and is frequently used as an indicator by health professionals, is that body fat that accumulates around the abdomen (creating the so-called 'apple' shape) is linked with more risk to health than fat elsewhere – e.g. on the hips or thighs. People with a large waist measurement are more at risk of heart disease, insulin resistance and diabetes than others of the same weight but a lower waist measurement.

So if you are an overweight 'pear shape', that is less of a problem than if you are an overweight 'apple'. If you are an 'apple' with thin arms and legs and/or little in the way of muscle, your weight on the scales may be deceptively low, so this waist measurement test is of particular value to you.

The Body Mass Index test

Although it has its detractors, the body mass index (BMI) test is still used all over the world as a fairly reliable way to tell whether individuals are underweight or overweight.

To find out your own body mass index you will need a calculator. First convert your weight into kilos (divide your weight in pounds by 2.2). Then find out your height in metres (multiply your height in inches by 0.025). Now square that height (e.g. 1.60 metres x 1.60 metres is 2.56). Finally divide your weight in kilograms by your squared height in metres and the result is your body mass index.

Here is a worked example:

→ You weigh 12 stone, which is 168 pounds. Divide this by 2.2 to get your weight in kilos, which is 76.36kg.
→ You are 5ft 6ins tall, which is 66ins. Multiply this by 0.025 to get your height in metres, which is 1.65m.
→ Square your height. 1.65m squared (1.65 x 1.65) is 2.72.
→ Now divide your weight in kg (76.36) by your squared height (2.72).
→ The result is 28, which is your BMI.

The BMI categories are as follows:

UNDER 18.5: UNDERWEIGHT

This means that you are clinically underweight and shouldn't attempt to lose any more weight. You may be at increased risk of various health problems, including malnourishment; in women this could mean cessation of periods, osteoporosis and other health problems. You may need to put on weight. I advise you to visit your GP who should put you in touch with your community dietician for advice.

18.5–24.9: NORMAL WEIGHT RANGE

This means that you come within the wide range of weights that can be classed as 'average' or 'normal'. If you are within this weight range, you should suffer no health problems because of your weight.

It is sometimes said that the actual 'ideal' weight for men is around BMI 22 and for women around 23. And it is often true that young healthy adults have a BMI towards the low end of this scale, and older healthy adults have a BMI towards the higher end – proving the point that it is almost 'normal' to put on some weight as you get older.

If your BMI is no more than 22 for men or 23 for women, I suggest that you don't need to lose any weight.

If you are within the normal range but still feel you are overweight, it may be that you just need to do more exercise to tone your muscles and firm up your appearance.

If you are towards the top end of the normal range, and have a large waist circumference (see page 72), you probably do need to lose a few pounds and take more exercise.

25–29.9: OVERWEIGHT RANGE

This means that, while you are not at more than slightly increased risk of health problems, you *are* overweight. You should probably aim to reduce your BMI to no more than 25. If you are in the upper range of this category, around 28–29, you should at least aim to slim down to a BMI of around 26 or 27. Coupled with a large waist circumference (see above), this BMI range should give you cause for concern.

Note: If you are particularly muscular you may find that you register in this group while not having a higher than average body fat percentage, because muscle weighs more than fat. Try the waist circumference test, which is more accurate in your case.

30–34.9: OBESE

This means that you are officially obese (very overweight) with substantially increased risk of health problems associated with your weight. You should aim to slim down to a BMI below 30 as a starting point, and then take another check. Reducing your weight by as little as 5 per cent could improve your health profile.

OVER 35: OBESE CLASS 2

You are extremely overweight, and the more overweight you are, the higher the health risks. You should aim to slim down to a BMI of 30 as a starting point and then take another check.

OVER 40: OBESE CLASS 3

You are extremely obese; in fact, you are what is sometimes classed as 'morbidly obese'. This means you are at risk of early death. You should aim to lose weight and my advice is that you should do this with the help of your doctor and community dietician.

Note: For convenience there is an instant BMI reckoner in the Appendix (see page 270). This works out your approximate BMI without the need for a calculator as long as you know your height and weight.

Question 2: How does the Traffic Light Diet work to help me lose weight without calorie counting?

No diet, the Traffic Light Diet included, can help you to lose weight without restricting your calorie intake somewhat.

The Traffic Light Diet limits your total calorie consumption by altering the balance of foods at each meal. Let's look at this in more detail.

The diet tells you to eat *less* – and sometimes much less – of the RED foods such as foods high in saturated fat, trans fat and sugar, which are generally high in calories. And it asks you to eat *more* of the GREEN foods such as fresh fruit, salads and vegetables, which are generally low or lowish in calories. Your intake of the AMBER foods, which tend to be moderate in calories, is kept at a reasonable level of around **six** small to medium portions a day excluding drinks and condiments.

So at a typical meal you will be cutting calories without actually calorie counting.

As we are aiming for slow or steady weight loss, you need to eat on average only around 500 calories a day less than you did on the diet that made you put on weight. The fairly moderate changes to your diet that are part of the Traffic Light system will easily achieve that.

As long as you sensibly follow the guidelines, you will lose weight.

Question 3: What do I do if my weight loss slows down or stops?

Assuming that you still do have weight to lose – and at this point it is worth rechecking your waist circumference and your body mass index (see Question 1) to see whether or not that is the case – you need to bear in mind the following points:

→ **The nearer you get to your target weight, the slower the weight loss will naturally be. This is because, in general, the lighter you are (whether or not you have ever been overweight) the less you need to eat to maintain your current weight. So, as you slim down and become lighter, you need to slightly reduce your calorie intake in order to continue to lose weight. The alternative is to take more exercise to burn off more calories (see Chapter 7) or a combination of the two.**

So for most people the best solution to this slowing down of weight loss is to just accept that the nearer you get to target, the slower the loss. There is no great hurry, is there? Especially as most research shows that the more slowly you lose the weight, the more chance that it will stay off. If you reduce your food intake too much, you will become dispirited, could become malnourished and stand less chance of succeeding in the long run.

→ If your weight loss actually stops altogether before you are at your target weight, first you need to ask yourself whether your target is actually set too low. For many older people a BMI of around 24–25 is low enough and anything much below that becomes too hard to achieve.

As we get older our metabolic rate begins to slow down. Some of these factors can be altered by hard work (e.g. more aerobic exercise, more weight-bearing exercise) but you can't compensate completely for this slowing down.

For young people (in their twenties and thirties), a BMI of 20–23 is plenty low enough. We tend to see stick-thin models and actors on the TV and think that we should look like that too – but it isn't the case. Often these so-called role models have to virtually starve themselves to stay so thin. In real life, it really doesn't look good. And, of course, it doesn't do you good either.

→ Lastly, you need to look carefully at what you eat and drink. Ask yourself whether you might be cheating or, at least, letting things slide! Are you still keeping a close eye on the amount of RED foods that you eat? Are you taking regular exercise to help create a calorie deficit? Cut your RED food intake for a week, take more activity and you will probably see the weight starting to move off again. If this doesn't work, you need also to look at the amount of AMBER foods you are eating. Are you sticking to the daily amount recommended for your circumstances? (See Question 7.)

I recommend weighing yourself a maximum of once a fortnight because continual scale-hopping will only lead to disappointment as you near your target weight.

Question 4: I have problems in my life that make dieting difficult – what advice do you have?

'It is vital that the psychological and behavioural aspects of obesity are addressed ... there are a multitude of reasons why people may overeat, many of them linked to underlying psychological factors.'

So says the Commons *Obesity* report, which goes on to record a fairly long list of reasons given by the people who were interviewed for overeating or not being able to diet. These include:

→ **Boredom, guilt, anger, stress, frustration.**
→ **Loneliness, tiredness, unhappiness, depression.**
→ **Feeling unloved, unfulfilled, unsatisfied, unappreciated.**
→ **Happiness, habit, holiday time, celebration time, Sunday.**
→ **Pressure from others, food availability.**

The trouble is that at least some of these factors are present in all our lives. We have worse problems at some times than others. If you are going through a particularly hard or bad time it may not the best moment to begin a new eating regime.

However, you need to ask yourself whether you really are having a 'bad patch' or, being truthful, whether you can always come up with a reason not to try to lose weight.

The Traffic Light Diet will work – but only if you want it to. So you need to do two things:

1. Really want to lose weight.
2. Accept that it is your responsibility to do so.

A third could be added:

3. Accept that there will always be lifestyle and emotional problems (well, there certainly are for most people) and that you can still eat healthily through these.

All the people I have helped to lose weight have done it, despite problems including divorce, death in the family, redundancy, depression, holidays, constant travelling, crippling shyness, loneliness and incredible stress levels. Importantly, they all felt that eating a healthy diet increased their self-confidence and actually helped them to deal with their problems.

Lack of time

One of the main reasons given by people without any obvious life problems who say that they can't lose weight is that they are just too busy.

When we lead busy lives – and few people don't – we have to prioritise. Sadly, diet is often one of the things that gets relegated to the bottom of the priority pile. The busier we are, the worse our diet becomes – more fast food, more junk food, less time spent shopping and in the kitchen, less time spent actually eating and enjoying food ... I believe this is very sad because food is one of the great pleasures of life and as such should be a priority, not an afterthought. And, of course, food is us – the food we eat becomes a lot of what we are, so it is also an important tool for health and well-being. Whether or not you need to lose weight, I am 100 per cent certain that you should make time for food and not resent it.

Having said that, you *can* eat fast as well as healthily. The Traffic Light Diet offers you a simple way to lose weight without calorie counting.

If you need quick and easy options when you are truly time-short, you can find them – for example, salads, cold cuts, cheeses, pasta, bread, cereals, milk, yoghurt, fresh fruit, seafood. All these are truly convenience foods. The menu plans for singles and couples offer a selection of quick and easy meals, and the recipes include many easy suppers. You can also choose time-saving options at the supermarket, such as ready-prepared vegetables, ready-mashed potato, ready-cooked rice and bagged, ready-mixed and washed salads.

So lack of time is not a particularly valid reason not to lose weight.

My advice? Get organised – decide what you are going to

eat in advance, make a weekly shopping list and stick to it. Reorganise your priorities if necessary to give yourself a few minutes extra a day for food preparation. For example, you decide to turn off the TV instead of watching a boring programme because it happens to follow the one you switched on for. If you really want to, I promise that you can find a few extra minutes in the day.

Lack of funds

People often say to me that dieting is expensive, and I always say that it shouldn't be. If you look down the lists of GREEN and AMBER foods in the diet (pages 30–39), you will see that they include many foods that are on the lower end of the cost scale; grains, pasta, bread, potatoes and pulses are all inexpensive. Many of the protein foods such as eggs, basic cheeses and chicken are not expensive, while if you choose fruits and vegetables in season they can be a reasonable price.

Obviously if you choose luxury foods such as lobster or oysters, and out of season produce such as strawberries in January, then it will cost you. But that is your choice.

Remember that you are cutting back on what are sometimes termed 'value added' products – i.e., commercially made products that make a big profit for the manufacturers. I think that commercial desserts, cakes, puddings, chocolate bars, crisps and so on are quite expensive for what you actually get – so you are saving money that way.

Question 5: I want to follow a diet but my tastebuds are just so tuned to sugar and fat – not to mention salt! Any advice?

Yes – the good news is that you can wean your tastebuds off all three in a matter of weeks.

It takes only two weeks to lose the taste for salty foods. To tackle added salt (e.g. in cooking vegetables or at table), simply reduce the amount you eat by a few grains a day until you are doing without it altogether.

Have courage and begin the Traffic Light Diet, and then try this experiment. When you have followed a low-salt diet for a few weeks, add to your food as much salt as you used to. You will feel like spitting it out – it tastes disgusting!

It is a similar story for sugar. Reduce the added sugar (e.g. in tea) in your diet little by little and start the Traffic Light plan. Sugary foods are mostly in the RED group – of which you are allowed tiny amounts, so you don't have to give up sugar altogether. However, here again you will find within weeks that if you have been eating the Traffic Light way, you will no longer find high-sugar foods palatable.

The Traffic Light Diet swops saturated and trans fats for other, healthier, fats – so you needn't miss fat in your diet. Most of the fat that you probably eat at the moment is so enjoyable because it is combined with either salt or sugar in various forms.

The Traffic Light plan clears your palate, renews your tastebuds and helps you to appreciate the natural flavours of real food – not manufactured rubbish.

Question 6: Dieting is boring – how do we get round that?

I suppose it depends on which diet you choose. I don't believe that the Traffic Light Diet is boring. It offers plenty of choice and variety. You aren't forced to eat things you don't like, and you aren't forced to give up anything you really crave.

There are menu plans and plenty of easy recipes to choose from.

I don't think that real food is boring; I can think of nothing better than preparing a supper with brightly coloured vegetables and good-quality fish or meat, or an array of spices for a Thai curry, or a plate of succulent fruits with thick yoghurt ...

You do need to get your tastebuds back into gear – and the only way you can do that is to follow a diet of *real* food for a few weeks.

It's up to you – and see the previous question.

Question 7: How many AMBER food portions can I eat a day while slimming?

Because this is a fairly 'free and easy' diet, which assumes that you are a sensible person, the amount of AMBER foods that you can have a day isn't written in stone.

In Chapter 2 I have suggested that a good level for female dieters who have less than three stone to lose, which should achieve steady weight loss, is around **six** small to medium portions of AMBER foods a day, excluding the AMBER drinks and AMBER condiments.

If you have more than three stone to lose, you may need up to **eight** portions a day in order to achieve steady weight loss rather than too-fast weight loss. (The heavier you are, the more you can eat and still lose weight.)

Male dieters and teenage girls may also need up to **eight** portions a day. Teenage male dieters may need even more.

People's needs also vary in other ways. For instance, your age (the older you are, the fewer AMBER portions you may need), and your activity levels (the more activity you do, the more AMBER portions you may need) have a bearing on how many calories a day you can eat and still lose weight. The best plan is to start off on one of the levels outlined above, then reassess your progress as follows:

→ **If you are losing weight at a steady rate – about one pound a week after the first couple of weeks on the diet (when weight loss is always quicker) – then continue on this level. If weight loss slows down, reduce your number of AMBER portions by one a day, and so on.**

→ **If you are losing weight too slowly – less than one pound a week – then reduce your number of AMBER portions by one a day. If this still doesn't work, reduce by a further portion. Also look at your activity levels (see Chapter 7).**

→ **If you are losing weight too quickly – more than 1.5 pounds a week – then increase the number of your AMBER portions by one a day. If the weight still continues to come off more quickly than 1.5 pounds a week, add another AMBER portion a day, and so on, until you reach the right dieting level for you.**

Question 24 supplies more information on ways to increase calorie intake on the diet for males, teens and females with a lot of weight to lose. In the Appendix on page 272 you will find a quick guide in chart form to the number of AMBER portions that different groups of people may require, both for dieting and weight maintenance.

Question 8: What quantity of the AMBER drinks can I have?

The AMBER drinks are coffee, green tea, white tea, black tea, oolong tea and pure fruit smoothies made with whole fruit at home (see recipes) and soda water.

You can drink all of these in moderation as an adjunct to your GREEN drinks, which include water, redbush tea, herbal teas and tomato and vegetable juices.

Assuming that your main source of drinks are GREEN ones, you could have two to three AMBER drinks a day, of your choice – preferably mixing them rather than having three all of the same kind.

Let's look at the drinks on the list.

Coffee contains caffeine, which should be limited in your diet. Large quantities of caffeine aren't good for health but most research shows that small amounts are OK. Unless you are pregnant or have breast pain, you can have a couple of cups of coffee a day with no problems. But try to avoid drinking coffee – and other caffeine-containing drinks – with a meal, as the caffeine can hinder the absorption of some of the nutrients in that meal.

Green, white, black and oolong tea all contain caffeine – but usually less than that found in coffee. They all also contain chemicals called polyphenols, which, research shows, can help protect you from heart disease. One or two cups of tea a day is sufficient to incur benefits to your health.

Pure fruit smoothies contain all the goodness of the whole fruit because, unlike juice extraction, all the solids and pulp – along with many plant chemicals, vitamins and minerals – aren't left behind. For this reason they are almost as good for you as whole fruit.

I say 'almost' because they do have some downsides. You will drink a smoothie much more quickly than you will eat whatever whole fruit went into the smoothie, thus you get none of the 'mouth action' that is useful in helping slimmers to feel satisfied. The smoothie will also take slightly less time for you to digest, because it has been broken down, and may thus cause a quicker rise in your blood sugar levels than would the whole fruit (see Chapter 1, pp 15–16). And lastly, they contain many more calories than you might imagine. This is because it takes several pieces of fruit to make enough smoothie to fill an average 300ml glass. A large smoothie can easily contain more calories than a fizzy canned sugary drink, for example.

However, a pure fruit smoothie now and then makes a welcome addition to the diet. You could also sometimes add some skimmed milk or low-fat bio yoghurt to the blender along with the fruit, which will give you added protein, vitamins and minerals – and which will help prolong the digestive period of the drink.

Why are tomato and vegetable juices on the GREEN list when fruit smoothies aren't?

That is because they are low in sugars and calories and very high in nutrients; also they don't impact on your blood sugar levels.

Soda water is carbonated water with the addition of sodium bicarbonate. Although calorie-free, it does contain sodium, so you shouldn't guzzle this drink. However, it can be used occasionally, half and half with a glass of white wine (see RED group) to make a spritzer.

Question 9: What quantity of the AMBER condiments can I have?

Condiments by their very nature are used sparingly. In the AMBER condiments list I have included items that aren't strictly condiments but which you may want to use in small quantities as a regular or occasional part of your diet.

Olive oil, a healthy oil high in monounsaturates, is the best oil to use for everyday cooking as it doesn't oxidise at high temperatures. If you use non-stick cookware and add just one tablespoon of oil for a recipe or dish that serves two to four people, you are not adding many calories to your overall diet. For this reason, you can do this once a day. When roasting, just brush the food items with oil rather than letting them sit in it.

You should also use olive oil as your main oil for salad dressings. Again, if you use just a tablespoon of olive oil French dressing (vinaigrette) on a salad that serves two people, you are adding just a few calories to your diet, so you can do this once a day too.

On days when you haven't used any olive oil for frying, roasting, etc. or in a salad dressing, you can add a little to vegetables once they are cooked, e.g. in mashed potato, or drizzled over greens. A very good-quality olive oil is also great when drizzled over a slice of plain good-quality bread. **Groundnut oil** and **sesame seed oil** are high monounsaturated alternatives.

Walnut oil is an alternative to olive oil for salad dressings or drizzling – use it instead of olive oil, not in addition.

Cooking oil spray, which can be bought in aerosols, delivers a very fine mist of oil, which you can use to coat frying pans, griddle pans and so on, to stop food from sticking when cooking. Use this spray whenever you like, certainly when you want to cook and have already used up your day's olive oil allowance.

All the other items on the condiments list can be used once or twice a day as necessary in small quantities. For example, you could put a couple of tablespoons of semi-skimmed coconut milk in a curry dish, or have a dollop of tomato ketchup with your supper if you want to.

If you use these condiments more often than twice a day

in total, your calorie intake will begin to creep up – and some of the items include higher than average levels of salt or other less desirable ingredients. I haven't included salt itself as a condiment and I would prefer you not to add any to your food, either in cooking or at the table. Spices, such as black pepper, you will remember, are GREEN foods.

Question 10: What are the best choices from the AMBER carbohydrate lists?

The AMBER carbohydrates include a wide variety of cereals, grains, breads and other items. They are an important part of most people's diets and you will find that on the diet plans in this book they form up to half of your daily AMBER portions.

Not all carbs are created equal. Sugar is a carb but that appears only on the RED lists. All other forms of carbohydrate are **starches**. White bread, white pasta and white rice are starches that have been produced using highly refined grains. The refining process removes some of the nutrients, as well as most of the fibre. For this reason I would prefer you to eat these foods in their whole-grain forms – whole-grain bread (rye, and other varieties as well as wheat), wholewheat pasta and brown rice.

Of the rices, **basmati rice** is one of the best to choose as it helps keep your blood sugar levels more even than other rices. Both brown and white basmati rice is available. If you are going to choose white rice, basmati white is definitely the best, but brown basmati has a delicious flavour and is very easy to cook, so do try it.

Oats are a good starchy carbohydrate food and, like basmati rice, will keep your blood sugar levels even more than many other types of grain, helping to stave off hunger pangs and to lower LDL cholesterol too. Eat plenty of muesli, porridge, oatbread and oatcakes. Your porridge should be the traditional kind, not the instant kind for preference, although instant oats are acceptable.

Pot barley is a top-notch grain. It is rich in soluble fibre (to lower cholesterol) and insoluble fibre (to help digestive problems and constipation), and is a good source of iron and protein as well as, like basmati rice and oats, being kind to blood sugar levels. Pot barley is the 'whole grain', whereas pearl barley is its poor cousin, where the nutrient and fibre-rich outer husk has been removed. You can make some excellent stews and soups using pot barley. In a similar way, traditional couscous (available from health food shops) is greatly superior to instant couscous, which is ubiquitous and which just needs soaking to reconstitute.

You have to be careful with **breakfast cereals**. Even if you choose whole-grain varieties, the label will show that they contain quite a lot of salt and even sugar. Oat-based muesli is a good choice as it contains other nutritious items such as nuts and seeds and rarely has added salt. Because of the additions, and because it contains less air than 'puffed' cereals, muesli is, weight for weight, quite a lot higher in calories than the other cereals on my list, therefore you should give yourself only smallish portions.

The cereals I have listed under AMBER (see page 38) are some of the best around, being high in nutrients, fairly unadulterated and reasonably low in salt and/or sugar.

When choosing starchy carbohydrate foods, try to vary your choices as much as possible, including different types of grain, not just wheat.

Question 11: How can I tell if a ready meal is RED or AMBER?

If you choose a ready meal that has a single-serving maximum of 10g fat, it will be AMBER. Try to pick ready meals that have a good fibre content – at least 6g fibre per serving – and which contain vegetables. If your chosen ready meal doesn't contain vegetables, you should serve it with two portions of vegetables or a large mixed side salad.

Try not to choose ready meals more than a couple of times a week, as they tend to be high in salt and the balance of fats they contain may not be ideal. Portions also tend to be quite small, so you may quickly get hungry again afterwards. Bulking the meal out with plenty of GREEN vegetables is the best idea – and finish with a piece of fruit.

Question 12: Would it be best to buy organic foods?

I am a fan of organic food and I would say that, if you can afford the extra, it is worth buying at least some organic foods. If you have to choose just a few, go for organic fish, meat and poultry, because the taste and texture are usually superior and you are buying more peace of mind. I buy all my meat and poultry from local farmers because then I know where my meat comes from, which I think is even more important than the organic factor. One point to mention here is that on the Traffic Light Diet you eat moderate or small portions of meats, etc., so by cutting down on the amount that you eat, you may be able to afford to spend extra on organic or locally farmed versions.

I would buy organic leafy greens and salad greens –

because it is nearly impossible to wash off residues from the huge amount of surface of these items, and because you can't peel them to remove residues either. In government tests, lettuces are most often likely to have higher levels of residues than is desirable.

Organic bread, nuts and seeds are a good idea because, again, flour, nuts and seeds have a huge surface area, which can contain high levels of pesticides and other residues.

The rest really is up to you. As I said earlier, food is such an important part of our lives that I think it is worth trying to get the best you can afford even if it means cutting back elsewhere.

Question 13: RED foods are allowed in small amounts but can you give me some further guidelines?

The Diet Plans in Chapter 3 show daily examples of how you can use the RED foods within your diet. For example, you can see that on most days there is a 'RED extra' included in the diet, which might be a 'treat' item like a glass of wine, some chocolate or a dessert or cake. Guidelines to maximum portion sizes for these items appear in the Food Reference Charts in Chapter 6. You should have no more than one portion of one of these items a day.

Then within the menus there are small amounts of other RED items, such as Cheddar cheese, sugar, honey, butter, low-fat spread, mayonnaise, jam and so on. A good guideline for these is to have no more than one at any meal. For more information on what constitutes a very small amount of these are, see the Food Reference Charts, but in general use your common sense.

A few examples:

→ hard cheese – 1 matchbox-sized chunk or 1 heaped table-spoon of grated cheese
→ sugar, butter, low-fat spread – 1 teaspoon
→ honey, jam – 1–2 teaspoons
→ mayonnaise – 1 dessertspoon

When you have reached your target weight and are eating for weight maintenance, you can increase your amounts of RED foods a little – either by increasing the number of times you eat them by about 25 per cent but having the same portion sizes, or by increasing portion sizes by about 25 per cent.

Question 14: Is there a best way of incorporating the RED foods into my diet?

Apart from the guidelines above, you should try to make sure that the RED foods are eaten as part of a meal rather than as items on their own. And you should not choose RED 'treat' items such as chocolate, cakes or desserts when you are hungry. Because they are high in sugar they tend to play havoc with your blood sugar levels and you may find yourself on the bottom step of the ladder towards a full-scale binge.

If you eat these foods at the end of a meal, this won't happen.

If you follow the diet properly, you should find over a period of several weeks that your taste for the sweet RED foods diminishes. You will also find that if you come back to them after a break of even a week or so, they taste much, much sweeter and less pleasant than you remember.

Question 15: Why is there so little alcohol allowed on the diet?

A good rule of thumb for alcohol intake is that it should account for no more than 5 per cent of your daily calories. As a RED extra, you can have daily up to one glass of wine (or a similar amount of other alcohol), which is around 100 calories. For most people losing weight steadily on this diet, this will represent approximately 5 per cent or a little more of their daily calories.

When you finish slimming and begin a maintenance programme, your calorie intake will increase a little but my advice is that you should still limit yourself to one glass of wine or similar a day. Alcohol can be a good thing for some people in small quantities (e.g. for older people, a glass a day – particularly the darker drinks such as red wine, stout and malt whisky – can have a protective effect for the heart) because of the polyphenols that most varieties contain. But apart from that, alcohol, which contains sugar and other additives, will add unnecessary calories to your diet for no nutritional benefit.

You should have your alcohol in the evenings only, and never drink without eating a proper meal.

That said, a glass of wine with a meal is a great way to relax and wind down at the end of a day. Being completely teetotal is not necessary on the Traffic Light Diet – unless you want to be.

Question 16: What sort of chocolate do you recommend?

Good-quality plain chocolate containing a high percentage of cocoa solids (over 50 per cent) is actually quite good for you and is my chocolate of choice. Cocoa beans contain plant chemicals called flavonols, which are powerful anti-oxidants and can help prevent heart and circulatory disease. A 40g bar of plain chocolate has the same protective effect as a glass of red wine. Plain chocolate is also quite a good source of the important minerals magnesium and iron.

So if you choose plain, you can eat your chocolate treat and not have to feel too guilty about it! However, like milk and white chocolate, plain chocolate still contains a high percentage of fat and sugar (although it is lower in cholesterol than milk chocolate), so it isn't all good news.

Good-quality chocolate, because of its protein and fat content, doesn't impact on blood sugar levels too strongly unless you binge. As we've seen, it does contain some nutrients, so is thus a much better choice for those with a sweet tooth than most other confectionery.

Question 17: Why do you advise avoiding all sweets apart from chocolate?

Much of what you see on the confectionery counters and in the sweet shops is true junk food. Most sweets are little more than sugar and artificial additives such as colourants and flavourings. There is no nutritional benefit; they can cause tooth decay and gum disease; they play havoc with your blood sugar levels; and they encourage a craving for sickly sweetness, which can be nothing but bad news for people trying to watch their weight.

Please just give them a miss!

Question 18: Why do you suggest avoiding all fizzy drinks and squashes including those labelled 'low in calories'?

Fizzy sweet drinks and squashes have a similar profile to confectionery (see above). Like sweets, they are basically nothing but water, sugar and a whole load of artificial additives.

As for 'diet' soft drinks and carbonated drinks, they also contain nothing of any use to you. Yes, they are low in calories and so in theory might help your slimming campaign, but I believe they simply encourage you to continue having a sweet tooth and there is no research to show that they actually do help overweight people to slim down. As to the idea that these drinks help fill you up and prevent hunger – well, a glass of water will do the same.

If you can abandon all fizzy and soft drinks and get a taste for pure water or some of the better teas, then you will be doing yourself, your diet and your health a favour.

I am not a big fan of any of the products – drinks or otherwise – that contain artificial sweeteners.

Question 19: Why are fruit juices on your list of RED foods?

Both fruits and fruit juices are high in sugar. When you eat the whole fruit, the sugar in that fruit is classed as 'intrinsic' – this means that it is a natural part of the cellular structure of the food. As such, it does not tend to raise blood sugar levels as quickly as sugars that are classed as 'extrinsic' – such as sugars added by you to foods, or added in manufacture ... or in fruit juices.

Because fruit juice contains virtually no protein or fat, only carbohydrate, those extrinsic sugars give you a very quick 'hit', rather like eating a bag of boiled sweets. So they are actually worse in many respects than eating a slice of fruit cake (for example), which, because it contains protein and fat, will take much longer to digest and will thus help keep the blood sugars more stable.

When you are consuming fewer calories than normal as you lose weight, it really is vital to try to keep your blood sugars on an even keel in order to avoid hunger pangs, to control appetite, and to stop you from feeling dizzy or lethargic.

There are other reasons to keep fruit juice drinking to a minimum. Fruit juices are much higher in calories than people realise and 'go down' so quickly. If you ate the equivalent in whole fruit instead, it would help keep hunger at bay, provide fibre and more of the important chemicals found in fruits, and save you lots of calories. Drinking fruit juice also contributes to tooth decay.

Recent research published in the *American Journal of Clinical Nutrition* found that those who consumed the most fruit gained less weight and body fat than those who consumed less fruit, but this finding related only to whole fruit and not fruit juice.

Question 20: Can I add salt to my food?

As we are probably all aware now, we do eat far too much salt in this country. We consume on average at least 9g a day, while we should try to get this level down to 4–6g a day (for adults – children need even less).

There is a direct link between high salt intake and high blood pressure, heart disease and stroke. Salt is also linked to asthma and osteoporosis. In addition a diet high in salt can also cause fluid retention – especially around the stomach – which can ruin the way you look even when you are losing weight.

The Traffic Light Diet, being high in natural foods such as fresh fruits and vegetables and low in processed and manufactured foods, helps you to reduce your salt intake without trouble. (Remember that 75 per cent of the salt we eat has already been added to the food that we buy, rather than what we add to it ourselves.)

Because the Traffic Light Diet is generally low in salt, I don't ban the use of salt in recipes, for cooking vegetables and so on – but I do advise that you use as little as possible. You will get all the salt you need in the diet from foods such as bread, breakfast cereals, sauces, etc.

As you saw in Question 5, it takes only a short time to lose the taste for salty foods, even when it comes to salting the cooking water for vegetables. For the first week on the diet, unsalted potatoes will taste really, really bland – but a couple of weeks later you will realise that potatoes taste just great as they are, without the need for added salt.

In the recipe section (Chapter 5) salt is not listed in the recipe ingredients with very few exceptions, but if you must add a pinch, that is up to you. Try not to add salt at the table – and always taste foods before adding salt anyway.

Question 21: Why are some of the GREEN foods bad for you in large quantities?

In the introduction to Chapter 2, in the section on 'GREEN for Go' foods, I say that you should aim to vary your choices from the GREEN items and not have a surfeit of just one or two, because even healthy items can be 'bad for you' in quantity.

This mainly refers to certain fruits and vegetables. Here are some of the ways that a surfeit can affect you badly:

➜ A surfeit of carrots can give you carotene poisoning.
➜ A surfeit of plums, oranges and several other fruits can give you stomach cramps and/or diarrhoea.
➜ A surfeit of certain vegetables such as cabbage, onions or artichokes (this varies from person to person) can cause bloating and 'wind'.
➜ A surfeit of pulses can do the same.

Even too much water taken all at one go can be bad for you by diluting the body salts too much. And it is well known that most vitamins and minerals have an official limit set on daily intake, above which they may be toxic. It would be unusual to overdose on vitamins and minerals on a healthy balanced varied diet unless you were to take supplements as well – but it *would* be possible.

So be sensible about your choices. Just because something is good for you it doesn't mean that too much is even better! The healthiest diet is a varied one.

And by the way, if your previous diet has been very short on fresh fruits, vegetables and pulses, you may need to increase the amounts you eat gradually so as not to give yourself indigestion or a loose bowel.

Question 22: If fish is such a healthy food, why are many varieties not in the GREEN group?

In the UK few of us consume enough fish for good health, and certainly not enough oily fish. White fish is a high-protein, low-fat food containing important B vitamins, iodine and selenium, and it is eminently suitable for a slimming and weight-maintenance diet.

Following a recent (June 2004) report from the Scientific Advisory Committee on Nutrition (SACN), the Food Standards Agency advises that we should all eat at least one portion of white fish a week. As there is no upper limit given (apart from one or two important exceptions – see below), these fishes appear in the GREEN group. You can eat as much as you like of them – but in practice, as with all the GREEN foods, and with any diet, variety is the key. So as part of your overall balanced diet you will probably not be eating white fish more than three or four times a week.

Oily fish, such as salmon, trout, herring and mackerel, is high in omega-3 fatty acids, regular consumption of which is important to help prevent heart and circulatory disease. These omega-3s have many other health benefits. Sadly, because much of the oily fish that we eat is contaminated with pollutants called dioxins and PCBs (polychlorinated biphenols), which are byproducts from industry that are found throughout the environment and in the sea, there is a limit on how much oily fish we can eat without being put at risk of health problems from these contaminants, which can accumulate in our bodies over time.

Pregnant women, women intending to become pregnant and girls are particularly vulnerable.

Recommended intakes of oily fish

Following the SACN report, the Food Standards Agency has given the following recommendations on oily fish consumption in the UK:

→ **Everyone should eat at least one portion of oily fish a week. One portion equals 140g. (Our current average intake is** about 50g a week although much of the population eats no oily fish at all.)

→ Girls and women who may have children one day, women who are either pregnant, intending to become pregnant, or breastfeeding should have *no more than two* portions of oily fish a week.

→ Women who are not intending to become pregnant in the future, boys and men can eat *up to four* portions of oily fish a week.

Other official recommendations on fish

In addition to this advice, there is more specific advice for particular groups and particular fish, as follows:

→ Because of the high levels of mercury they may contain, shark, marlin and swordfish should be avoided altogether by women who are either pregnant or are intending to become pregnant, and children under the age of sixteen.

→ Other groups should limit themselves to *one portion a week* of these three fishes.

→ Canned tuna should be limited to *four medium cans a week* by women who are either pregnant or intending to become pregnant. Canned tuna does not count as an oily fish.

→ Fresh (or frozen) tuna should be limited to *two portions a week* by women who are either pregnant or intending to become pregnant. Fresh or frozen tuna does count as an oily fish.

The reason for the limits on tuna is that it also contains levels of mercury higher than in most other fish, although not as high as in shark, marlin and swordfish.

Lastly, if you love oily fish and want to eat it up to your recommended limits, be aware that the levels of dioxins and PCBs vary from one type of oily fish type to another.

(Unfortunately figures are not available for all types of oily fish.)

→ **Herring tends to contain high levels.**
→ **Salmon and mackerel tend to contain intermediate levels.**
→ **Trout tends to contain lower levels.**

After all that, to answer your question as to why all the fish are not in the GREEN group, it is because you need to limit your intake of some, due to possible health problems.

But please don't be put off increasing your intake of fish up to the safe levels for you as described above. The FSA says that eating just one portion of oily fish a week has clear-cut health benefits.

So, once again, it is all about moderation and balance in your diet. For an at-a-glance guide to minimum and maximum levels of fish for different groups, see Appendix, page 273.

Question 23: How can I follow the Traffic Light system when eating out?

It isn't difficult to apply the GREEN–AMBER–RED system to most meals that you'll encounter when eating out although there will be less choice in certain types of restaurant than in others.

Here are some examples:

→ **Small steak (AMBER), large mixed salad (GREEN), olive oil dressing (AMBER), new or baked potato (AMBER); fresh fruit salad (GREEN); cream (RED extra).**
→ **Roast chicken (AMBER – remove skin), two or three portions of vegetables (GREEN), new or baked potato (AMBER); cheese (RED extra) and oatcake (AMBER).**

→ Garlic mushrooms in tomato sauce (AMBER); Greek lamb on the bone (AMBER), selection of Mediterranean vegetables (AMBER), the oil used for cooking these items counted as your RED extra.

→ Medium pasta portion (AMBER), sauce of seafood and tomato (AMBER, because of the olive oil content), green side salad (GREEN), a little Parmesan (RED extra).

In general, composite dishes such as curries and lasagnes, and dishes cooked with a cream or butter sauce, are probably RED dishes because they are likely to be high in fat and calories. All deep-fried foods will be RED. Plainer dishes such as grills, roasts, bakes are likely to be AMBER. For carbs, plain rice, potatoes and bread are on most menus and can be chosen instead of chips, pasta or fried rice. Or you could skip the carb element of the meal and just go for protein and vegetables – you can make up your carbs at another time in the day.

If you choose a vegetable-based starter, such as soup or melon, and a fruit-based dessert, you will be on fairly safe ground and then can eat one or two small RED extras such as a little cream or butter without having to worry.

You can always ask the waiter how a dish is cooked if you aren't sure.

Bear in mind that you should aim for medium portions rather than super-sizes – so avoid dining at places where portions do tend to be huge, such as a pizza parlour or a pasta house, unless you can take somone with you and share! If you want pasta, consider choosing a pasta starter dish as your main course.

Most of us don't eat out all that often. If it is a rare occasion for you, there is no need to be too strict on yourself. If you have to eat out a great deal for work and have a busy social life too, you need to pay more attention to what you order on each occasion.

Question 24: Do the menus and recipes listed contain enough calories for men or teens who need to lose weight?

Any portion guidelines given in the diet plans are for female dieters with less than three stones to lose, and children aged between five and eleven who need to watch their weight, so dieting teens and men (and, of course, non-dieting members of the family and women with over three stones to lose) will need to increase the calorie content of the diets. This can be done easily and most healthily by increasing the number of AMBER portions in the daily diet.

For female dieters with less than three stones to lose, I have recommended up to six portions of AMBER foods a day on average. I suggest that males, teens and women with more than three stones to lose should increase this to around *eight* portions a day. This is easily done in one of the following ways:

1. By adding AMBER items to meals – for instance, a slice of bread to a lunch or to a recipe meal (one portion of a recipe meal is suitable for a female dieter with less than three stones to lose).
2. By doubling up AMBER items when stated (e.g. if the diet plan states one small to medium portion of basmati rice, it should be doubled in size to one large portion).
3. By adding on extra AMBER snacks between meals. This can be items such as a small piece of Brie and an oatcake; a pot of whole-milk bio yoghurt; a handful of sunflower seeds; a few nuts; a handful of dried fruit.

Obviously to these extras can be added any extra items as liked from the GREEN lists.

For anyone using the Traffic Light Diet to lose weight, it is best not to use the RED foods to increase calorie intake, but stick to the amounts given in the basic diets.

Some teen and male dieters, and women with more than three stones to lose, may need *more than eight* AMBER portions a day. If you are losing weight at a rate of more than 1.5–2 pounds a week, you should add on extra AMBER portions until your weight loss slows down to the right level.

Teenagers and males who are *not dieting* will almost certainly need to add on even more AMBER portions to the daily menus (see the next question and Question 29 on weight maintenance).

Question 25: What changes to the Traffic Light Diet plans do non-dieting members of the family have to make?

People who don't need to lose weight are in essence the same as people who have been slimming and now need to follow a maintenance diet. Therefore they should increase the AMBER portions in their diet and follow the other guidelines as explained in Question 29. Non-dieting females, and children, will probably need between eight and ten AMBER portions a day, while non-dieting teens and males may need around ten or more.

Because the system is so flexible, non-dieters can use the basic GREEN–AMBER–RED Traffic Light guidelines on pages 29–43 to devise their own diet.

Question 26: Why is the diet not suitable for children under five?

I say that the diet is not suitable for children under five because young children have special dietary needs. For example:

→ They should not be given whole nuts and seeds.
→ They may not be able to eat more than small amounts of fresh fruit and vegetables (their small digestive systems may not be able to cope).
→ They should have smaller amounts of some items like oily fish.

Other foods should be avoided for children under the age of one – for example, honey, uncooked eggs, soft cheeses.

For more information on pre-school childhood nutrition, go to the Food Standards Agency website (www.fsa.gov.uk)

However, most of the general principles of the Traffic Light Diet do and should apply to pre-school-age children – particularly the avoidance, most of the time, of the foods in the RED category. No child, no matter what their age, needs a diet that contains bright, artificially-coloured fizzy drinks, sweets that contain sugar, additives and little else, snack foods that provide nearly a whole day's sodium intake in one bag – and so on.

Once a child begins to be weaned, you should help them develop a taste for wholesome, nutritious foods rather than junk.

Question 27: Is the diet suitable for diabetics and those with heart disease or cancer?

The diet is a healthy one, which should make it particularly suitable for diabetics and also for those with heart disease and cancer. However, if you are ill or have been diagnosed with any disease, it is always advisable to consult your doctor about your diet and take the advice of any dietician to whom you may be referred.

Alternatively, you may like to show your health professional this book and ask whether the diet is suitable for you. The answer will probably be yes but if you are receiving medical treatment you should always follow the professional's advice for your own case.

The nutritional needs of people convalescing, after surgery or during treatments such as chemotherapy is a specialist area.

Question 28: Is the diet suitable during pregnancy and breastfeeding?

The Traffic Light system is a healthy one, which in general is suitable during pregnancy and breastfeeding as long as you take into account the list of 'foods to avoid' below. The diet plans for singles, families and couples, however, are slimming-level diets and do not contain enough calories for women who are pregnant or breastfeeding.

You should therefore follow the general guidelines on pages 29–43 but devise your own diet to include enough calories to ensure your own health as well as that of the foetus during pregnancy, and your health and that of the baby while you are breastfeeding. The maintenance diet on pages 62–69 may be suitable for the first few months of pregnancy but consult your GP first.

Interestingly, pregnant women only need extra calories (about 200 more a day) in the last three months of their pregnancy. Research indicates that when you are pregnant the metabolic rate slows down and the body makes better use of all the nutrients it receives. So 'eating for two', in terms of calorie intake, is not strictly necessary. (It is when you are breastfeeding that your calorie needs increase quite substantially; around 500 extra calories a day are required to feed an infant solely on breast milk.)

If you are pregnant but overweight you should talk to your doctor about what might be done about this. Don't try to follow a slimming diet of any kind unless you have been told to do so by your health professional and are monitored throughout.

In pregnancy you need adequate folate. The Traffic Light plan contains a lot of folate-rich foods but you should still take a supplement.

You also need a diet with adequate calcium – so make sure to eat plenty of low-fat, high-calcium foods (low-fat yoghurt, skimmed milk and nuts for example). You also need adequate iron (dark leafy greens, lean red meat, whole grains). One portion of oily fish a week will help to ensure healthy brain development of the baby.

Foods to avoid during pregnancy

→ You should try to avoid alcohol and choose drinks low in caffeine.

→ You should avoid soft cheeses such as Brie and Camembert, as well as unpasteurised cheeses, such as Parmesan, and blue-veined cheeses, such as Stilton.

→ You should avoid pre-packed salads and any loose-sold, chilled-cabinet items.

→ You should avoid raw or lightly cooked eggs and anything made with them, including mayonnaise.

→ You should avoid meat pâtés and all liver products because of their high vitamin A content.

→ You should avoid shark, marlin and swordfish, and limit your intake of tuna (see Question 22).

Question 29: What tips do you have for following the Traffic Light system for weight maintenance?

Why does the weight so often come back after you have lost it? Many people go wrong because they go back to eating in the way that caused them to gain weight in the first place.

What is so good about the Traffic Light system is that it doesn't leave you 'in the lurch' with no idea of what kind of diet to follow, now that the slimming is over. You can follow it to provide a healthy balanced diet for the rest of your life.

A sample of a week's maintenance eating (the Traffic Light Maintenance Diet) appears on pages 62–69 in Chapter 3. Give it a try when you are down to the weight you want to be. After that, for variety you need to devise your own eating plan. It isn't hard. All you do is follow the basic Traffic Light system using the GREEN–AMBER–RED groups on pages 29–43, but slightly increase the amount of AMBER foods that you eat, compared with the amount that you ate while you were slimming, to a point where your weight remains steady. For most people this will represent an increase in your calorie intake of around 25–30 per cent.

Increasing AMBER foods

You can increase the amount of AMBER foods you have in three ways:

1. By adding AMBER items to meals – for instance, a slice of bread to a lunch or to a recipe meal (one portion of a recipe meal is suitable for a female dieter with less than three stone to lose).
2. By increasing the portion sizes of AMBER foods. To start with, try increasing them by around 25 per cent and a little further if necessary .
3. By adding on extra AMBER snacks between meals. This can be items such as a small piece of Brie and an oatcake; a pot of whole-milk bio yoghurt; a handful of sunflower seeds; a few nuts; a handful of dried fruit.

You can also have slightly higher amounts of the AMBER condiments.

In all, most people who need to maintain their weight will be eating around ten portions of AMBER foods a day but this obviously depends on how much you increase portions sizes and other factors. Men and teenagers will, in general, be able to eat more than women and children. The easy way to tell whether you are eating the right amount for you is to check that your weight remains stable, about once a fortnight.

There is a quick 'at a glance' AMBER portions chart for different groups of people in the Appendix on page 272.

Increasing RED foods

You can also very slightly increase the amount of RED foods that you have, either by eating them a little more frequently or by slightly increasing portion sizes. If surplus weight ever starts to return again, immediately cut back on these RED items to 'slimming' levels.

And, of course, you eat all you like of the GREEN foods.

You can add in recipes from Chapter 5, and devise some of your own, referring to the Food Reference Charts in Chapter 6 for further detail on any particular food.

That's it really – and, of course, don't forget to keep up with a regular programme of activity (see Chapter 7). It is well documented that people who exercise regularly are most successful at maintaining their weight loss.

Remember that although you most definitely don't have to eat 'slimming' rations for the rest of your life in order to stay slim, if you go back to the eating and exercise habits that you had when you were overweight, the weight will probably return.

5 RECIPES

There are over forty recipes in this chapter, all based on the guidelines for healthy – and weight-conscious – eating that we've been discussing in the previous chapters.

All the recipes contain a wide variety of the GREEN foods, moderate amounts of the AMBER foods and some-times, but not always, small portions of some of the RED foods.

There is no nutrition information given on the recipes as all are both healthy and suitable as part of a slimming or weight-control diet. Each recipe has tips on those for whom it might be particularly suitable: vegetarians, slimmers, novice cooks, couples, etc.

In all cases, people who need more calories than is pro-vided by one portion of the recipe (strapping, non-dieting teenagers, for example!) can add extra AMBER foods to their plate (e.g. more bread, pasta, rice, potatoes) or follow the dish with a dessert or snack.

I have tried to ensure that all the recipes are easy to cook, in that they are either quick to prepare and cook, or can be left to look after themselves. And of course they have to be delicious to eat. Look out for the 'Tips' box at the end of many of the recipes, offering ideas on how to adapt or vary them.

Many recipes appear in one or more of the diet plans in Chapter 3. When they do, there is a cross-reference to the appropriate diet plan and the day on which it is used.

Most are low or moderate in cost and need no special equipment other than what most people have in their kitchens already. Because we are keeping additional fat low or low-ish, it would be a good idea, if you don't have some already, to buy some good-quality, heavy-based, non-stick pans as well as a couple of similar quality baking/roasting tins, to help prevent food sticking and to ensure even cooking without burning. If any particular equipment is needed, this is indicated at the top of the recipe.

Note 1: Recipes serve either two or four, depending upon the recipe (this information is shown at the top of individual recipes). Many can be adapted to serve fewer or more people by reducing or increasing the amounts of ingredients appropriately.

Note 2: Salt does not appear in the ingredients lists apart from the Trout Fillets with Almond Pesto and the Mediterranean Vegetable Pizza, but if you wish to add a little salt to the savoury recipes, that is up to you. Try to keep any added salt to a minimum and always add it at the end of cooking time.

Soups and Snacks

QUICK SPICY LENTIL SOUP
Serves 2

Particularly suitable for: novice cooks, slimmers, singles, vegetarians
Ideal for: winter, hearty lunch, light main meal

Used in: Singles Plan, Day 3 and Day 7
You will need: an electric blender (optional)

---

1 tablespoon olive oil
1 medium onion, peeled and chopped
1 medium carrot, peeled and chopped
1 teaspoon harissa paste (see Tip)
freshly ground black pepper
1 large tomato, chopped *or* 100g canned chopped tomatoes
150g green lentils (dry weight)
500ml low-salt vegetable stock (made using cube or bouillon)

Heat the oil in a large non-stick saucepan and sauté the onion and carrot for 2–3 minutes to soften, stirring occasionally. Add the harissa paste and pepper, and allow to cook for 1 minute, stirring, until the aroma of the spices is released. Add the tomato, lentils and stock, and stir well to combine. Bring to a simmer, cover and cook for 30 minutes or until the lentils are tender (check).

Allow the soup to cool slightly, then transfer to a blender and whizz for 1 minute until almost smooth, but with a few small chunks remaining. Return to the pan, adding a little more stock or water if the mixture looks too thick and reheat. Check seasoning and serve.

 Tips
• Moroccan harissa paste contains chilli and other spices, and is available in small jars in the supermarket.
• If you don't want to blend the soup, it is just as good with the small chunks and whole lentils.
• The soup looks attractive when garnished with fresh coriander or flat-leaf parsley.

CHUNKY VEGETABLE AND BEAN SOUP
Serves 4

Particularly suitable for: budget cooks, families, novice cooks, vegetarians
Ideal for: winter eating, main meal
Used in: Family Plan, Day 2

1–2 tablespoons olive oil
1 large onion, peeled and finely chopped
2 medium sticks celery, chopped
1 medium leek, cleaned and sliced
1 large carrot, peeled and chopped
1 medium potato, peeled and chopped
200g spring greens, cleaned and finely sliced
200g can chopped tomatoes
1 level tablespoon sun-dried tomato purée
1 litre low-salt vegetable stock
1 bouquet garni
1 x 400g can cannellini or butter-beans
freshly ground black pepper

Heat the oil in a large non-stick saucepan and add the onion, celery and leek. Stir-fry for 2 minutes to soften over a medium heat. Add the carrot and potato, and stir for another 2–3 minutes. Next add the greens, tomatoes and tomato purée, and stir well to combine. Add the stock and the bouquet garni, stir again and bring to a simmer. Cover and simmer for 20 minutes.

Meanwhile, drain the beans into a bowl. When the simmering time is up, add half the beans to the pan as they are. Mash the remainder in the bowl with some black pepper, and add to the pan. Bring back to a simmer.

Cook for another 5 minutes and serve.

Tips

- Bouquet garni is a small sachet of mixed herbs, available from most supermarkets. As an alternative use some sprigs of fresh thyme, parsley and oregano.
- For an even heartier soup for non-vegetarians, add some chunks of chicken fillet (no skin) at the same time as the carrot and potato.

RED LENTIL AND SQUASH SOUP
Serves 4

Particularly suitable for: families, novice cooks, vegetarians
Ideal for: autumn eating, lunch
Used in: Family Plan, Day 4
You will need: an electric blender

1–2 tablespoons olive oil
1 large onion, peeled and finely chopped
1 medium clove garlic, crushed (optional)
200g red lentils (dry weight)
1 medium butternut squash, peeled and cut into 1.5cm cubes
1 level teaspoon ground cumin seed
half a level teaspoon ground coriander seed
800ml low-salt vegetable stock
200ml skimmed milk
freshly ground black pepper
fresh coriander leaves

Heat the oil in a large non-stick saucepan and add the onion and garlic, stirring over a medium heat for 2–3 minutes to soften. Add the red lentils and squash with the ground cumin and coriander seed. Stir for 1 minute to coat everything well and release the aroma of the spices.

Add the stock, milk and some black pepper. Bring to a simmer, turn down the heat, cover and simmer for 30 minutes or until the lentils are tender (check).

Allow to cool slightly, then pour the soup into an electric blender (you may have to do this in two or three lots) and blend until smooth. Return the soup to the pan, reheat gently and serve garnished with fresh coriander leaves.

 Tips

- If you have time you could brush the squash cubes with olive oil and roast them in the oven for 20 minutes or so until lightly golden, before adding them to the soup. This will increase its flavour.
- You can make a similar soup using carrots instead of the squash, although remember to cut the carrots into smaller pieces, as otherwise they will take longer to cook.

SUMMER VEGETABLE SOUP WITH CRUDITÉS
Serves 2

Particularly suitable for: couples and singles, vegetarians
Ideal for: late spring and summer lunches
Used in: Couples Plan, Day 2

---

1 tablespoon groundnut oil
medium bunch spring onions, cleaned, most of dark green top removed and chopped *or* 4 shallots, peeled and sliced
4 baby carrots, washed and sliced
1 small courgette, topped, tailed and thinly sliced
100g small fresh shelled peas
100g small fresh shelled broad beans
4 vine tomatoes, roughly chopped

few fresh mint leaves, finely chopped
350ml low-salt vegetable stock
1 level tablespoon mint sauce (see tip)
2 tablespoons ready-made garlic croutons

Heat the oil in a large non-stick saucepan. Add the spring onions or shallots, carrots and courgette, and stir-fry over a medium heat for 2 minutes to soften. Add the peas, broad beans, the tomatoes (with all their juices and pips) and the chopped mint, and stir for 1 minute.

Now pour in the stock, stirring. Bring to a simmer and cook for 15–20 minutes or until the vegetables are just tender. To serve, drizzle half the mint sauce over each bowl of soup and finish with the croutons.

 Tips

• If you prefer, you can use frozen petit pois and broad beans (thawed).

• The vegetables can be varied according to what you have.

• You can add some fresh chopped parsley to the soup if you like, with the mint.

VICHYSSOISE
Serves 4

Particularly suitable for: budget cooks, novice cooks, vegetarians
Ideal for: summer lunches
Used in: Maintenance Plan, Day 2
You will need: an electric blender

---

1 tablespoon groundnut oil
1 small knob butter

1 medium onion, peeled and finely chopped
2 large or 4 small leeks, cleaned, trimmed and thinly sliced
1 large potato (about 250g), peeled and chopped
800ml low-salt vegetable stock
200ml skimmed milk
freshly ground white pepper
fresh chives or parsley to garnish

Heat the oil and butter in a large non-stick saucepan. Add the onion and leeks, and stir-fry over a medium heat for 2–3 minutes to soften. Add the potato and stir to combine, then add the stock, milk and pepper. Bring to a simmer, turn down the heat, cover and cook over a low heat for 30 minutes or until all the vegetables are tender.

Allow to cool slightly, then tip the soup into an electric blender (you may need to do this in two or three lots). Blend until smooth. Either cool the soup completely in the fridge to serve cold (as is traditional) or reheat gently to serve hot. Garnish with chives or parsley.

 Tips

- If you have not used or are allowed some RED items, add a dash of cream to each bowl.
- A similar soup can be made omitting the leeks, doubling the quantity of onion and adding one large bunch of trimmed watercress to the pan with the potatoes.

RED PEPPER SOUP
Serves 4

Particularly suitable for: vegetarians
Ideal for: summer lunches, dinner party starter

Used in: Maintenance Plan, Day 3
You will need: an electric blender

1–2 tablespoons olive oil
4 large red peppers, deseeded and finely chopped
1 large clove garlic, peeled and well crushed
1 mild red chilli, deseeded and finely chopped (optional)
1 tablespoon ready-made red pesto (see Tip)
freshly ground black pepper
500ml passata (see Tip)
200ml water or vegetable stock
dash of balsamic vinegar (see Tip)
fresh flat-leaf parsley to garnish

Heat the oil in a large non-stick saucepan. Add the red peppers and stir-fry over a medium heat for 2–3 minutes to soften. Add the garlic and chilli, and stir for another minute. Add the pesto and black pepper, and stir well to combine. Pour in the passata and water or stock, and bring to a simmer. Turn down the heat and simmer, covered, for 20 minutes or until the peppers are tender (check).

Allow to cool slightly, then pour the soup into an electric blender and blend until smooth. The soup should have a consistency that pours easily. If it looks too thick, add a little more water or vegetable stock and blend for a few seconds more.

Return to the saucepan and reheat gently, adding a dash of balsamic vinegar. Garnish with flat-leaf parsley to serve.

Tips
- If you can't find any ready-made red pesto (usually found with the sauce jars in the supermarket), add sun-dried tomato paste instead.
- Passata, sold in jars or cartons, is simply puréed and sieved tomato.
- You could also use red or white wine vinegar instead of balsamic.
- For a slightly more robust soup, add 2 tablespoons ground almonds to the soup after blending, stirring in well.

HUMMUS
Serves 4

Particularly suitable for: vegetarians
Ideal for: all-year-round snacks, buffets, dips, flatbread filling, mezze, starters
Used in: Singles Plan, Day 4; Maintenance Plan, Day 1 and Day 7
You will need: an electric blender (ideal but not completely necessary)

1 x 400g can chickpeas, drained
juice of 1 lemon
2 tablespoons olive oil
1 level tablespoon light tahini
1 large clove garlic, peeled and well crushed
freshly ground black pepper
a little water

Tip the chickpeas into the electric blender and add the lemon juice, olive oil, tahini, garlic and pepper. Blend until smooth, adding 1 tablespoon of water at a time until you have a thick purée. Spoon out into a bowl and chill before serving.

 Tips

- If you don't have a blender, simply mash everything together thoroughly in a mixing bowl.
- A traditional recipe uses up to 100ml olive oil, making it extremely high in calories. My recipe uses less oil, with the addition of water to make the purée.
- Tahini is a delicious and healthy sesame seed paste, available in jars from the supermarket. Stir well before using as all the oil rises to the top.
- If you thin hummus with a classic vinaigrette, it makes a lovely dressing for salad, pasta or bulghur wheat.
- Leftover hummus can be covered and kept in the fridge for a day or two.

GUACAMOLE
Serves 4

Particularly suitable for: vegetarians
Ideal for: all-year-round snacks, dips, sauce, toast topping
Used in: Family Plan, Day 3

2 medium tomatoes
2cm piece cucumber
1–2 large cloves garlic, peeled and very well crushed
1 mild green chilli, deseeded and finely chopped
dash Tabasco
juice of 1 good lime
2 large ripe avocados
handful chopped fresh coriander leaves

Make a cross on the stalk end of the tomatoes and blanch them in boiling water for 1 minute, or microwave for 30 seconds. Peel off the skin, halve and deseed. Chop the flesh into a large bowl. Peel, halve and deseed the cucumber, and finely chop the flesh, then add to the bowl together with the garlic and chilli, Tabasco and lime juice. Combine well.

Now peel, stone and chop the avocados, and add to the bowl. Mix together well with a large fork or wooden spoon. If the avocado is suitably ripe, you should find that it easily forms a purée. Stop mixing while a few small lumps of avocado are still visible, to add texture.

Stir in the coriander leaves, cover and refrigerate. Serve chilled.

 Tips
- You need really good ripe avocados.
- You can omit the cucumber if you are in a hurry.
- You can omit the chilli and/or Tabasco for a mild version.

CANNELLINI BEAN DIP
Serves 4

Particularly suitable for: couples, vegetarians
Ideal for: dips, sandwich filler, toast topping
Used in: Couples Plan, Day 6
You will need: an electric blender

---

1 x 400g can cannellini beans, drained
1 large clove garlic, peeled and well crushed
1–2 tablespoons olive oil
juice of half a lemon

freshly ground black pepper
small handful fresh flat-leaf parsley or fresh basil, chopped

Put all the ingredients except the herbs into the electric blender and purée for a few seconds. If the mixture is too stiff (see Tips), add a little water and blend again.

Stir in the herbs, then transfer to a bowl, cover and refrigerate. Serve chilled.

 Tips

- For a sandwich filling, the mixture needs to be firmer than for a dip.
- You can use butter-beans instead if you like – they are from the same family.

Salads

CHEESY COLESLAW
Serves 4

Particularly suitable for: families, vegetarians
Ideal for: cold meat accompaniment, sandwiches
Used in: Family Plan, Day 1

200g white cabbage (see Tip)
1 medium to large carrot, peeled
1 small onion, peeled
50g Cheddar cheese
50g sultanas
2 tablespoons low-fat natural bio yoghurt
2 level tablespoons reduced-calorie mayonnaise
a little lemon juice

freshly ground black pepper
a little skimmed milk as necessary

Grate the white cabbage, carrot, onion and cheese into a large mixing bowl. Add the sultanas and combine well. In a small bowl, mix together the yoghurt, mayonnaise, lemon juice and black pepper, adding enough skimmed milk to make a dressing just thin enough to pour. Pour this over the vegetables and stir thoroughly to combine. Cover and refrigerate. Serve chilled. This will keep in the fridge for a couple of days.

 Tips
  • You can use a combination of red and white cabbage if you like.
  • You can use chopped ready-to-eat dried apricots instead of the sultanas for a change.

WATERMELON AND CRISP PARMA HAM SALAD
Serves 2

Particularly suitable for: couples, slimmers
Ideal for: dinner party starter, light lunch, summer lunch
Used in: Couples Plan, Day 5

100g pack Parma ham
cooking oil spray (see Tip)
300g slice watermelon, peeled
2 good handfuls rocket leaves
1 tablespoon olive oil French dressing (see Tip)

Coat a medium non-stick frying pan with several sprays of

cooking oil spray and add the slices of Parma ham in one layer. Cook over a medium heat until the Parma ham begins to cook and become crisp. Turn each slice over and cook the other side.

Remove the ham from the heat when it is all crisp but not completely solid.

Meanwhile, cut the watermelon into bite-sized cubes and arrange on two serving plates with the rocket leaves. When the ham is ready, sprinkle it over the melon and drizzle the French dressing over the top. Serve immediately.

 Tips

- Cooking oil sprays are usually to be found near the oils at the supermarket.
- You can buy a good-quality, ready-made French dressing, or make a simple one of your own by combining 4 tablespoons olive oil with 1 tablespoon red wine vinegar, a dash of balsamic vinegar, half a teaspoon French mustard, half a teaspoon caster sugar, freshly ground black pepper and a couple of grinds of sea salt. Combine thoroughly. Leftovers will keep in a covered container for a considerable time. To make more, simply double or quadruple the quantities.

SALAD NIÇOISE
Serves 4

Particularly suitable for: families
Ideal for: hearty lunch or summer supper
Used in: Maintenance Plan, Day 1

---

heart of a cos lettuce
300g new potatoes, cooked and allowed to cool
75g French beans, cooked

4 small fresh (or frozen and thawed) tuna steaks
8 cherry tomatoes
4 tablespoons olive oil French dressing (see Tip previous recipe)
4 medium hard-boiled eggs (see Tip)
4 medium spring onions, finely chopped
8 stoned black olives, halved
a handful of fresh flat-leaf parsley, chopped

Tear the outer leaves of the lettuce heart into bite-sized pieces and cut the centre into quarters. Arrange on a serving platter or in a shallow bowl. Cut the new potatoes into bite-sized pieces if necessary and arrange them on the lettuce together with the French beans.

Griddle or grill the tuna steaks for approximately 90 seconds per side, then separate with a fork into bite-sized chunks and arrange on the salad. Halve the cherry tomatoes and arrange around the dish, then evenly drizzle over the French dressing.

Peel and quarter the eggs and arrange on top of the salad. Finally garnish with the spring onions, black olives and parsley. Serve immediately.

 Tip
• Unless this is for pregnant women, the very young, the elderly or anyone else who should not eat raw or partly cooked eggs, it is very nice if you can leave the eggs with a little runniness in the centre.

PESTO CHICKEN SALAD
Serves 4

Particularly suitable for: families
Ideal for: buffet dish, hearty lunch or summer supper

Used in: Maintenance Plan, Day 4

200g wholewheat pasta shapes, e.g. farfalle or shells
2 large or 3 small cooked chicken breast fillets (skin removed)
2 level tablespoons good-quality, ready-made basil pesto
2 level tablespoons olive oil French dressing
10 cherry tomatoes, halved
1 level tablespoon chopped sun-blush tomatoes
1 heaped tablespoon pine nuts, toasted
4 large spring onions, chopped
good handful fresh basil leaves

Cook the pasta in plenty of boiling water according to the packet instructions. Meanwhile, slice each chicken breast diagonally into eight. Set aside. In a serving dish, combine the pesto with the French dressing.

When the pasta is drained and cooled but still a little warm, tip it into the serving dish and combine thoroughly with the dressing. Stir in the cherry and sun-blush tomatoes, half the pine nuts and half the spring onions. Arrange the chicken slices around the dish, garnish with the remaining pine nuts and spring onions, and the basil leaves, and serve.

 Tip
• The salad is just as good without the chicken, either for vegetarians or as a side dish for other meats.

BROAD BEAN, COURGETTE, FETA AND MINT SALAD
Serves 4

Particularly suitable for: families with older children, slimmers, vegetarians

Ideal for: buffet, mezze platter

300g fresh broad beans (see Tip)
3 medium courgettes
2 tablespoons olive oil
juice of 1 lemon
200g feta cheese
good handful fresh mint, finely chopped
freshly ground black pepper

Boil the broad beans for 2–3 minutes until tender. Set aside.

Preheat a griddle pan or grill. Slice the courgettes diagonally to the thickness of a pound coin, and toss them in 1 tablespoon of the olive oil. Put them on the very hot griddle or under the preheated grill, and grill until golden – or striped if using a ridged griddle pan – on one side. Turn and grill the other side until golden and tender. Arrange in a serving dish and sprinkle over half the lemon juice.

In a separate bowl, toss together the broad beans, feta, mint, remaining lemon juice, black pepper and remaining tablespoon of olive oil, and combine with the courgettes. Serve immediately.

 Tip
- Frozen broad beans can be used. Whatever kind you use, make sure they are small and tender.

SALMON, AVOCADO AND ROCKET SALAD
Serves 4

Particularly suitable for: maintenance dieters
Ideal for: buffet, summer lunch or supper

400g salmon fillet
several large crisp salad leaves, e.g. cos or romaine
1 packet rocket leaves
2 large avocados
2 tablespoons olive oil
juice of 1 lime
freshly ground black pepper
1 tablespoon pine nuts, toasted

Grill, microwave or poach the salmon fillets for 2–3 minutes until they are cooked but still slightly pink in the centre. Remove any bones and skin, and flake the flesh into a bowl. Set aside.

Arrange the salad leaves (tear the larger ones as necessary) with half the rocket on a serving platter. Arrange the salmon flakes on top. Halve, stone and peel the avocados, cut into slices crossways and then halve the slices. Arrange around the salmon together with the rest of the rocket. Mix together the olive oil, lime juice and black pepper, and sprinkle over. Before serving, garnish with the pine nuts.

 Tip

• This salad is high in fat but almost all of them are 'good for you'– omega-3s in the salmon and pine nuts, and monounsaturates in the avocado, olive oil and pine nuts. It is also rich in vitamin E.

Main Meals – Meat and Poultry

BEEF AND TOMATO CASSEROLE
Serves 4

Particularly suitable for: families, novice cooks
Ideal for: freezing, autumn and winter suppers
Used in: Family Plan, Day 1

---

1 tablespoon olive oil
1 large or 2 medium-sized sweet onions (e.g. Spanish), peeled and thinly sliced
500g lean braising steak, cut into about eight pieces
1 x 400g can chopped tomatoes
2 large fresh tomatoes, roughly chopped
1 level tablespoon sun-dried tomato paste
150ml low-salt beef stock
1 bouquet garni
freshly ground black pepper
250g mushrooms, sliced

Heat the oil in a heavy non-stick flameproof lidded casserole and sauté the onions for 5 minutes to soften them. When they are beginning to colour slightly, push them to the edges of the pan and add the steak, in two batches, to brown on either side. When all the steak is browned, stir the pan contents to combine the steak and the onions. Add the chopped and fresh tomatoes with any juice, and the sun-dried tomato paste. Stir well to combine, then add the stock, bouquet garni and pepper.

Bring to a simmer and then turn down the heat, cover and cook gently, either on the hob or in a low (140°C/300°F/Gas 1–2) preheated oven, for 1¹/₂ hours. Add the mushrooms, stir, replace the lid and cook for a further 30 minutes. Serve hot.

 Tips
- You can use red wine instead of the stock, or half and half.
- This dish can be served with noodles or mashed potatoes and a selection of green vegetables.
- If freezing the dish, freeze at the point before you add the mushrooms. Thaw completely, add the mushrooms and reheat for 30 minutes. Ensure the dish is piping hot.

CHILLI CON CARNE
Serves 4

Particularly suitable for: families with older children
Ideal for: freezing, centrepiece winter buffet dish, winter suppers
Used in: Family Plan, Day 3

1–2 tablespoons olive oil
1 large or 2 medium-sized sweet onions (e.g. Spanish), peeled and chopped
450g lean braising steak, minced or cut into small pieces
1 large clove garlic, peeled and well crushed (see Tip)
2 medium red peppers, deseeded and chopped
2 medium-hot red chillies, deseeded and chopped (see Tip)
1 tsp Tabasco (optional)
1 x 400g can chopped tomatoes
1 level tablespoon sun-dried tomato paste
1 x 400g can red kidney beans (see Tip), drained and rinsed
250ml low-salt beef stock
handful fresh coriander leaves

Heat the oil in a large non-stick lidded frying pan and sauté the onions, stirring frequently, over a medium heat until they have softened and turned transparent. Turn up the heat to high, add the steak to the pan and cook for 2–3 more minutes, turning frequently, until the meat is all browned.

Add the garlic, peppers and chillies, and stir for another 2–3 minutes (if the mixture becomes too dry, add a little of the beef stock). Add the Tabasco (if using), the tomatoes, tomato paste, kidney beans and stock, and stir well to combine. Bring to a simmer, then cover and cook over a gentle heat for approximately 1¹/₂ hours. Serve hot, garnished with the fresh coriander leaves.

 Tips
- Garlic adds a depth of flavour without itself being detectable in the dish (in case you have children who don't like garlic!).
- If you like a very hot chilli con carne, add the chilli seeds to the pan.
- You can use black beans or other types of canned drained bean in this dish.
- Serve with basmati rice or baked potatoes and plenty of green salad. Guacamole, which smoothes down the chilli a little, is very good with it too.

GREEK MARINATED LAMB
Serves 2

Particularly suitable for: couples
Ideal for: dinner party, spring or summer
Used in: Couples Plan, Day 6

2 good-quality lamb steaks

1 juicy lemon
2 cloves garlic, peeled and well crushed
small handful fresh oregano leaves, chopped
few fresh thyme leaves
1 small sprig fresh rosemary, destalked and finely chopped
1 small glass dry white wine
1 tablespoon olive oil
freshly ground black pepper
2 large fresh tomatoes, halved and deseeded

Place the lamb steaks flat in a suitably sized non-metal baking dish. In a separate bowl, combine all the ingredients except the tomatoes, and pour over the lamb. Cover and marinate in the fridge for 3–4 hours or overnight.

Preheat the oven to 200°C/400°F/Gas 6. Cut the tomatoes into quarters and arrange round the lamb steaks. Baste the lamb and the tomatoes several times with the marinade juices. Cover the meat loosely with a piece of foil but don't seal it.

Bake in the preheated oven for 15 minutes. Remove the foil, baste again (adding a little water to the pan if the juices have dried out) and bake uncovered for a further 10 minutes. Serve hot.

 Tips

• Serve with couscous or new potatoes and green vegetables.

• If cooking this dish for more than two people, you can use a suitably sized leg of lamb and increase the cooking time appropriately (1 hour for a small leg, 2 hours for a large leg), reducing the temperature to 180°C/375°F/Gas 5.

TURKEY CHEESEBURGERS
Serves 4

Particularly suitable for: families, novice cooks, weight maintenance
Ideal for: barbecues, quick meals
Used in: Family Plan, Day 4

350g minced turkey meat
50g breadcrumbs (see Tip)
1 small onion, very finely chopped
handful fresh flat-leaf parsley, very finely chopped
l medium egg, beaten
half-teaspoon steak seasoning
freshly ground black pepper
1 dessertspoon groundnut oil
4 wholemeal baps
4 slices soft Italian mozzarella cheese
watercress, tomato and salad garnish

Place the turkey meat in a large mixing bowl and add the breadcrumbs, onion, parsley, egg and seasoning, stirring well with a wooden spoon to combine. Divide the mixture into four and, using your clean hands, form into round burger shapes.

Heat a griddle or non-stick frying pan and brush with the oil. When very hot, add the burgers and cook on high for approximately 5 minutes on each side. Check that the burgers are cooked all the way through by cutting a small slit in the centre of one with a sharp knife – if any pinkness remains, cook a little longer.

When the burgers are nearly ready, halve the baps and warm them in the microwave or toaster. To serve, place a burger on the base of each bap, cover with a slice of mozzarella (the warmth will melt it a little) and garnish with the salad items.

Tips
- The breadcrumbs should be made from fresh bread rather than bought ready-made, but ideally the bread should be slightly stale.
- A little reduced-calorie mayonnaise or some tomato ketchup can be added to the burger garnish, and/or slices of gherkin.
- Serve with plenty of salad or baked beans or green vegetables such as peas or green beans.

CHICKEN AND PRAWN SIZZLE
Serves 4

Particularly suitable for: couples, families with older children
Ideal for: all year round, dinner parties
Used in: Family Plan, Day 5

1–2 tablespoons groundnut oil
2 or 3 large or 4 small skinless chicken breast fillets, each cut into eight slices
1 good tablespoon sweet chilli sauce
350g packet ready-to-use Thai or Chinese stir-fry vegetables
juice of 1 lime
150g cooked tiger prawns
2 tablespoons ready-made satay sauce

Heat half the oil in a large non-stick frying pan or wok and add the chicken pieces. Stir-fry over a high heat for 2–3 minutes until they are virtually cooked, then add the sweet chilli sauce, the rest of the oil and the vegetables.

Stir-fry for 3 minutes or until everything is just tender. Add the lime juice, tiger prawns and satay sauce, and stir for 1 minute until really hot before serving.

Tips
- You can use raw prawns in the recipe if you can find them. Leave the tails on but remove the shells, and add at the same time as the vegetables.
- Serve with brown or white basmati rice, or rice noodles.

CHILLI FRIED CHICKEN WITH CORIANDER
Serves 2

Particularly suitable for: couples
Ideal for: quick supper, winter
Used in: Couples Plan, Day 1

1 supermarket container fresh coriander
1 large clove garlic, peeled and lightly crushed
2–3 teaspoons ready-crushed red chillies (see Tip)
1 teaspoon Thai fish sauce
juice of half a lime
2 tablespoons groundnut oil
2 'slabs' dried medium egg thread noodles (half a standard pack)
2 medium skinless chicken breast fillets, each cut into four slices on the diagonal
1 small packet baby corn cobs
1 fresh mild red chilli, deseeded and thinly sliced

Destalk the coriander and put half of it in a bowl with the garlic, ready-crushed chillies, fish sauce, lime juice and about a third of the groundnut oil. Set aside the remaining coriander. Using a wooden spoon or a pestle and mortar, pound the mix together until you have a very rough paste. Set aside.

Put a large pan of water on to boil. When it has boiled

add the noodles to the pan and cook according to the packet instructions. When they are cooked, drain out almost all of the water. Add a dash of groundnut oil, stir, cover and keep warm while you make the chilli chicken.

Heat a non-stick frying pan or wok brushed with a little more of the oil and, over a high heat, brown the chicken pieces all over, which should take about 4 minutes. Add the baby corn cobs with any remaining oil and stir for 3 minutes more. Tip the rough paste and the fresh sliced chilli into the pan and stir thoroughly to combine. Continue to stir-fry for another 1–2 minutes. Serve hot on the bed of noodles, garnished with the remaining coriander leaves.

 Tip

- You can find ready-crushed chillies in any supermarket but if you prefer you can use two whole hot red chillies, in which case chop them very finely.

CHICKEN, AUBERGINE AND GARLIC ROAST
Serves 2

Particularly suitable for: couples, maintenance dieters
Ideal for: summer, weekends

---

1 small aubergine, topped, tailed and cut into 1 cm rounds, then into halves
1 medium red onion, peeled and cut into six wedges
1–2 tablespoons olive oil
2 large chicken breast fillets (skin on), each cut in two
6–8 cloves new season's garlic, unpeeled (see Tips)
sprigs of fresh thyme or 1 teaspoon dried thyme
freshly ground black pepper
50ml (approx) low-salt chicken stock

Preheat the oven to 190°C/375°F/Gas 5. Brush the aubergine slices and onion wedges with the olive oil and arrange them in an ovenproof pan with the chicken pieces. Tuck the garlic cloves in between the vegetables and chicken, and sprinkle over the thyme and black pepper. Drizzle with 1 tablespoon of chicken stock and any remaining olive oil.

Roast in the preheated oven on a medium shelf for 30–40 minutes, basting at least twice during that time with the pan juices, and adding a little more chicken stock if the pan looks like drying out. You want to end up with about 1 good tablespoon of 'juice' per person. You should also turn the aubergine and onion halfway through so that they cook evenly and turn nicely golden.

Pierce a chicken piece and a slice of aubergine and onion to make sure that everything is cooked through (if the chicken is cooked, the juices will run clear and there should be no pinkness in the centre). Remove the skin from the chicken pieces and serve hot, with the pan juices drizzled over.

 Tips

• New season's garlic (available around late summer) roasts very well and is delicious to eat – just squeeze out the creamy interior of the clove. You could, if you like, combine the cooked flesh of half the garlic cloves with the pan juices to make a lovely garlicky sauce.

• This is good served with mashed or new potatoes and a green vegetable such as spinach or runner beans.

CARIBBEAN CHICKEN WITH RICE AND PEAS
Serves 4

Particularly suitable for: maintenance dieters
Ideal for: parties
Used in: Maintenance Plan, Day 1

---

8 skinless chicken thigh fillets
1 level teaspoon chicken seasoning
1 level dessertspoon Jamaican Jerk seasoning
1 clove garlic, well crushed
1½ tablespoons groundnut oil
200ml low-salt chicken stock
175ml skimmed coconut milk
1 x 400g can red kidney beans *or* mixed beans, drained and rinsed
225g white basmati rice (dry weight)
1 level teaspoon sweet ground paprika

Cut each chicken thigh fillet in half and place in a bowl. In a separate bowl, mix together the chicken seasoning, Jamaican Jerk seasoning, garlic and half the oil. Add to the chicken and combine thoroughly. Leave to marinate for 1 hour or more.

Heat the remaining oil in a large non-stick frying pan and sauté the chicken over a medium heat for 4–5 minutes until it is browned on all sides. Add the chicken stock to the pan. Bring to a good simmer, then reduce the heat and cook uncovered for 20 minutes, or until the chicken is tender and cooked through and the stock is reduced to around half.

While the chicken is cooking, bring a pan with the coconut milk and 300ml water to the boil. When boiling, add the rice and beans to the pan. Turn down the heat, cover and cook for 20 minutes, or until all the liquid is absorbed and the rice is cooked. Roughly fork the paprika through the rice.

Serve the rice in bowls, topped with the chicken and sauce.

 Tips
- This dish is good with a tomato and onion salad and a mild green salad.
- You can thicken the chicken juice a little if you like by stirring in 1 teaspoonful of sauce flour (see Tip on page 143) or cornflour for the last few minutes of cooking.
- As you will have noticed, the 'peas' in this dish are, in fact, beans.

Main Meals – Fish and Seafood

FAMILY FISH PIE
Serves 4

Particularly suitable for: all ages, maintenance dieters
Ideal for: autumn and winter, weekends
Used in: Family Plan, Day 7

600g floury potatoes, e.g. King Edwards, peeled and diced
knob butter
50ml semi-skimmed milk
1 teaspoon Dijon mustard
300g cod, haddock or other white fish fillet
200g salmon fillet
500ml skimmed milk
1 heaped tablespoon sauce flour (see Tip)

75g grated strong Cheddar
juice of quarter of a lemon
freshly ground white pepper
100g smallish mushrooms (not button), sliced
100g peeled prawns
good handful fresh curly parsley, finely chopped

Cook the potatoes in boiling water for 15 minutes or until tender when pierced with a pointed knife. Drain and mash with the butter, semi-skimmed milk and Dijon mustard.

Place the white fish and salmon in a non-stick frying pan and cover with the skimmed milk. Bring to a simmer and cook gently for about 5 minutes at most. Drain the milk from the pan and reserve. Separate the fish into large chunks and place in a pie dish.

Preheat the oven to 190°C/375°F/Gas 5. Strain the milk into a saucepan. Whisk in the sauce flour over a medium heat until the milk simmers and the sauce thickens. Add the cheese and stir until melted. Add the lemon juice and pepper.

Scatter the mushroom slices, prawns and parsley over the fish and then pour over the cheese sauce. Finally spread the mashed potato on top and fluff it up into peaks with a fork (this gives a larger surface area to turn crisp and golden).

Bake in the preheated oven for about 25 minutes. Serve hot.

Tips

• You can vary the fish that you use in this pie according to what is available and/or the best price. If you have not used up your egg allowance for the week, omit the prawns and replace with hard-boiled eggs instead. Alternatively, omit the prawns altogether.

• Sauce flour is a very fine flour, which can make a good white sauce without the addition of fat required to form a roux. You just need to keep whisking while the milk and flour heats up.

• Serve the pie with plenty of green vegetables such as peas and broccoli.

BROCHETTE OF MONKFISH AND PRAWNS
Serves 2

Particularly suitable for: couples, slimmers
Ideal for: barbecues, dinner parties, quick suppers
Used in: Couples Plan, Day 2
You will need: metal skewers or wooden brochette sticks

300g monkfish fillet
juice of 1 lemon
6 large raw crevette-type prawns (see Tip)
6 mushrooms approx. 2.5cm in diameter
2 rashers low-salt extra-lean back bacon, cut into bite-sized pieces
4 bay leaves
1 tablespoon olive oil
freshly ground black pepper

If using wooden brochette sticks, soak in water for 1–2 hours so that they won't burn under the grill.

Cut away any grey membrane from the monkfish fillet and then cut into 2cm cubes. If you have time, place the cubes in a non-metallic dish, sprinkle over half the lemon juice and allow to marinate for 1–2 hours.

Preheat the grill to high or a griddle pan over a high heat. Thread the monkfish cubes on to the wooden sticks, alternating with the prawns, mushrooms and bacon pieces, with a bay leaf in the middle of each brochette.

Brush everything with the olive oil, sprinkle with black pepper and cook for a total of approximately 6 minutes, turning at least once to ensure they cook evenly. When the brochettes are golden and sizzling, serve hot with the remaining lemon juice drizzled over and some more black pepper.

 Tips
- Serve with rice and a large salad.
- If you can't get raw prawns, omit them and use squares of red pepper instead.

TROUT FILLETS WITH ALMOND PESTO
Serves 2

Particularly suitable for: couples
Ideal for: quick suppers, summer
Used in: Couples Plan, Day 7
You will need: a small electric grinder; pestle and mortar (optional)

60g blanched almonds
2 tablespoons olive oil
good handful fresh basil leaves, torn if the leaves are large
1 clove garlic, peeled and lightly crushed

juice of 1 lime
fresly ground black pepper
small pinch coarse sea salt
cooking oil spray
2 medium trout, filleted
1 lime, quartered

First make the pesto. Place the blanched almonds in the electric blender and pulse for a few seconds (check regularly to ensure they are not over–processed). Tip into a small mixing bowl and add the olive oil, basil, garlic, lime juice, pepper and salt. Combine thoroughly with a wooden spoon, or use a pestle and mortar, until you have a rough paste. Set aside.

Heat a large non-stick frying pan. Spray with cooking oil spray and, over a medium heat, cook the trout fillets for approximately 8 minutes, turning once. When they are cooked through, drizzle over the remaining pesto. Serve hot, garnished with lime quarters.

 Tips
- It is always best to grind almonds yourself as the nutrients in the nuts deteriorate if they are bought in a packet, ready-ground, and stored for more than a few days.
- Serve with new potatoes and plenty of green vegetables or a large side salad.

COD WITH CHILLI TOMATO SAUCE
Serves 4

Particularly suitable for: families with older children, maintenance dieters, novice cooks, slimmers
Ideal for: all year round
Used in: Maintenance Plan, Day 7

---

1 tablespoon olive oil
2 large cloves garlic, peeled and well crushed
2 fresh chillies, deseeded and finely chopped
1 x 400g can chopped tomatoes
1 level tablespoon sun-dried tomato paste
2 tablespoons fresh chopped flat-leaved parsley
freshly ground black pepper
4 medium cod fillets (see Tip)
fresh flat-leaved parsley to garnish

Heat the oil in a medium non-stick lidded pan. Stir-fry the garlic and chillies for 1 minute, then add the chopped tomatoes, sun-dried tomato paste, parsley and pepper. Bring to a simmer, cover and cook for 10 minutes. Remove the lid and cook gently for a further 10 minutes or until you have a thick sauce.

Meanwhile preheat the oven to 180°C/365°F/Gas 4. Place the cod fillets on a non-stick baking tray. Spoon over the thickened sauce evenly to completely coat the fillets.

Bake in the preheated oven for 20 minutes, or until the fish is cooked through. Serve hot, garnished with a little parsley.

Tips
- You can use other fish fillets if liked, such as monk-fish or haddock.
- The tomato sauce can be made without the chilli and used in a variety of other recipes.
- Serve with pasta or potatoes and broccoli or other green vegetables.

HARISSA SWORDFISH WITH RICE AND LENTILS
Serves 4

Particularly suitable for: maintenance dieters, slimmers
Ideal for: winter

1–2 tablespoons olive oil
1 medium onion, finely chopped
1 half-teaspoon each ground cinnamon, turmeric and allspice
100g basmati rice
100g puy or green lentils (dry weight)
400ml low-salt vegetable stock
4 medium swordfish steaks
1 level tablespoon harissa paste (see Tip)

Heat the oil in a non-stick lidded saucepan and add the onion. Stir-fry for 2–3 minutes to soften, then add the ground spices and stir again. Tip in the rice and lentils, and stir well. In a separate saucepan, heat the vegetable stock. When hot, add to the rice and lentils. Bring to a simmer, cover and cook for 30 minutes, or until the rice and lentils are tender.

Towards the end of the cooking time, preheat the grill to medium. Brush the swordfish steaks on both sides with the harissa paste and cook under the preheated grill for approximately 8 minutes, turning once. Serve hot, with the rice.

> **Tips**
> • Harissa paste, a very hot Moroccan spice mixture, can be bought in jars from supermarkets.
> • Alternatives to swordfish in this dish are halibut or cod steaks.

Main Meals – Vegetarian

MEDITERRANEAN VEGETABLE PIZZA
Makes two individual pizzas

Particularly suitable for: couples, singles, vegetarians
Ideal for: weekends
Used in: Singles Plan, Day 6; Maintenance Plan, Day 5

150g strong white flour
pinch salt
half-teaspoon easy-blend yeast
100ml warm water
1–2 tablespoons olive oil
1 medium red onion, peeled and thinly sliced
1 medium red pepper, deseeded and chopped
1 medium courgette, topped, tailed and thinly sliced
1 clove garlic, peeled and well crushed
1 quantity Tomato Sauce (see Tip)
75g soft Italian mozzarella cheese
fresh basil leaves

Mix together the flour, salt and yeast in a bowl. Make a well in the centre. Gradually pour in the water and 1 tablespoon of the olive oil, mixing well with a fork to form a dough. Knead the dough on a clean, lightly floured work surface until it is smooth and elastic. Divide into two and set aside, covered, in a warm place until it has doubled in size – about 1 hour.

Meanwhile, heat the remaining oil in a non-stick frying pan. Add the onion, pepper and courgette, and stir-fry for 4–5 minutes until everything is lightly coloured, adding the garlic towards the end of the cooking time.

Preheat the oven to 220°C/425°F/Gas 7. When the dough is risen, knock it back and roll out into two circles on a clean, lightly floured work surface. Transfer the bases to a non-stick baking tray. Spread the tomato sauce evenly over the bases and spoon over the vegetable mixture. Finally slice the mozzarella and arrange on the vegetables together with some basil leaves.

Bake in the preheated oven for 20 minutes, or until the base is crisp and the top is bubbling and golden. Serve hot.

 Tips

• For a home-made tomato sauce, use the sauce recipe in the Cod with Chilli Tomato Sauce recipe (page 146), omitting the chilli. Alternatively, buy a 300g jar good-quality, ready-made thick tomato sauce.

• If you don't want to make your own pizza bases, you can buy ready-made packs of individual bases in most supermarkets, although they are higher in salt.

• You can vary the vegetable topping as you like – for instance, adding mushrooms or sliced artichoke hearts.

MEZZE PLATTER
Serves 2

Particularly suitable for: couples, novice cooks, vegetarians
Ideal for: hearty lunch or light supper, summer
Used in: Couples Plan, Day 3

---

1 x 200g can cannellini beans, drained and rinsed
half-quantity Tomato Sauce (see Tip), cooled
6 or 8 crisp, boat-shaped lettuce leaves, e.g. Little Gem
half-quantity Hummus (see recipe page 121)
2 wholemeal pittas, sliced
6 ready-made dolmades (see Tip)
4 cherry tomatoes, halved
100g halloumi cheese
lemon wedges

Combine the beans with the cooled tomato sauce and spoon portions on to several crisp lettuce leaves. Arrange the filled leaves on two serving plates alongside the hummus, sliced pitta, dolmades and cherry tomato halves. Cut the halloumi cheese into six slices and grill or dry-fry in a non-stick frying pan until golden, turning once. Arrange on the serving plates with the lemon wedges, and serve while the cheese is still warm.

 Tips
• You can use either the Tomato Sauce recipe (see the recipe for Cod with Chilli Tomato Sauce, page 146), or you could use a good-quality, ready-made tomato sauce for pasta.
• You can buy dolmades (rice-filled vine leaves) at the deli counter in most supermarkets.

PEPPERS STUFFED WITH HERB RICE
Serves 2

Particularly suitable for: couples, slimmers, vegetarians
Ideal for: light lunch or supper dish
Used in: Couples Plan, Day 5

---

1 tablespoon olive oil
1 medium-sized sweet onion (e.g. Spanish), peeled and finely chopped
1 clove garlic, peeled and well crushed
100g brown basmati rice
250ml low-salt vegetable stock
1 heaped tablespoon fresh mixed herbs, chopped
2 large red or yellow peppers, halved lengthways and deseeded, leaving stalk on
60g feta cheese, crumbled
2 good tablespoons sun-blush tomatoes, chopped
freshly ground black pepper

Heat half the oil in a non-stick lidded saucepan and stir-fry the onion for 2–3 minutes to soften. Add the garlic and stir for another minute. Add the rice and stir well. Pour in the vegetable stock and herbs, and bring to a simmer. Cover, turn down the heat and cook gently for 30 minutes, or until the rice is tender.

Meanwhile, preheat the oven to 190°C/375°F/Gas 5. Brush the peppers with the remaining olive oil, inside and out, and put on a baking dish. Bake in the preheated oven for 20 minutes. When the rice is ready, drain well and turn into a bowl. Remove the peppers from the oven, leaving them on the baking tray.

Stir the feta cheese, sun-blush tomatoes (with any juice) and pepper into the cooked rice, combining well. Pile the rice into the cavities of the peppers. Place a small piece of cooking foil over the top of each and return the baking tray to the oven for a further 15 minutes or until the peppers are tender. Serve hot.

 Tips

- If you can find them, use piquillo peppers, which have a fine taste and texture.
- Brown basmati rice has a nice nutty flavour and in my opinion is better than white for this dish.
- Sun-blush tomatoes are semi-dried tomatoes, available at supermarkets at the deli counter or in packets.

MUSHROOM AND NOODLE STIR-FRY
Serves 2

Particularly suitable for: vegetarians
Ideal for: quick supper
Used in: Maintenance Plan, Day 2

2 flat 'slabs' dry medium egg thread noodles
1 dessertspoon sesame oil
1 dessertspoon light soya sauce
1½ tablespoons groundnut oil
300g shiitake mushrooms, sliced (see Tip)
125g broccoli, cut into small florets
small knob fresh ginger, peeled and very finely chopped
1 clove garlic, peeled and well crushed
1 tablespoon yellow bean sauce
50ml low-salt vegetable stock
100g fresh beansprouts
small handful fresh coriander

Cook the noodles according to the packet instructions in a large pan of boiling water. Drain off almost all the water. Stir in the sesame oil and a little of the soya sauce. Cover and keep warm.

Heat half the groundnut oil in a non-stick frying pan and stir-fry the mushrooms and broccoli for 2–3 minutes. Add the ginger and garlic with the rest of the oil, and stir for another minute. Add the yellow bean sauce, the rest of the soya sauce and the vegetable stock, and stir over a high heat for 1–2 minutes. Stir in the beansprouts and cook for another minute. Finally stir in the coriander. Serve the vegetables immediately, on a bed of the warm noodles.

 Tips

- You can use any tasty firm mushrooms, such as chestnut or oyster, or a mixture.
- Non-vegetarians can add some sliced chicken or pork to the dish. Stir-fry the meat for 2–3 minutes before adding the mushrooms and broccoli to the frying pan.

SWEET POTATO BALTI
Serves 2

Particularly suitable for: vegetarians
Ideal for: quick dish, winter supper
Used in: Maintenance Plan, Day 3

---

1 large (about 400g) orange-fleshed sweet potato, peeled and cut into bite-sized cubes
60g fine beans, halved
100g cauliflower florets
1 tablespoon groundnut oil

2 shallots or 4 spring onions, finely chopped
1 level tablespoon balti curry paste
2 medium fresh tomatoes, chopped
100ml skimmed coconut milk
small handful fresh coriander

Parboil the potato, beans and cauliflower in a pan of boiling water for 2–3 minutes to soften. Meanwhile heat the oil in a non-stick frying pan and stir-fry the shallots or spring onions for 2 minutes to soften. Add the balti curry paste and stir for 1 minute.

Drain the vegetables and add to the frying pan, stirring well to combine, and cook over a medium heat for 2–3 minutes until they begin to colour. Tip in the tomatoes and coconut milk, stir again, bring to a simmer and cook for 15 minutes uncovered.

Serve hot, sprinkled with the coriander leaves.

 Tips
- Serve with basmati rice and a large side salad.
- Butternut squash can be used instead of the sweet potato.

SPINACH AND PINE NUT PASTA
Serves 2

Particularly suitable for: couples, novice cooks, vegetarians
Ideal for: all year round, quick supper

150g spaghetti or pasta shapes of choice (dry weight)
1–2 tablespoons olive oil
75g pine kernels
1 clove garlic, peeled and well crushed

1 x 200g bag baby spinach leaves
juice of 1 lemon
freshly ground black pepper
1 heaped tablespoon grated Parmesan cheese

Heat a large pan of water and cook the pasta according to the packet instructions.

Meanwhile, brush a non-stick frying pan with a little of the olive oil. Place on the heat, add the pine kernels in a single layer and toast until golden, taking care not to burn them. Turn them over when the undersides are done. Remove the kernels from the pan and set aside.

Add the rest of the oil to the pan. When it is hot, add the garlic and stir-fry for 1 minute. Add the spinach leaves and stir-fry to wilt them, adding the lemon juice and black pepper at the last minute.

When the pasta is cooked, drain well and turn on to serving plates. Stir in the spinach and pine kernels and serve, garnished with the Parmesan cheese.

 Tips
- You can use rocket instead of the spinach.
- Serve the pasta with a large mixed salad.

RATATOUILLE WITH POACHED EGGS
Serves 4

Particularly suitable for: vegetarians
Ideal for: hearty lunch or light supper
You will need: four ovenproof gratin dishes

2 tablespoons olive oil
2 medium red onions, peeled and sliced

3 mixed or red peppers, deseeded and sliced
3 medium courgettes, topped, tailed and sliced
1 medium aubergine, topped, tailed and sliced
2 cloves garlic, peeled and well crushed
freshly ground black pepper
1 level tablespoon sun-dried tomato paste
1 x 400g can chopped tomatoes
good handful fresh basil
4 large eggs

Heat the oil in a large, lidded non-stick frying pan and sauté the onions and peppers for 2–3 minutes over a medium heat, stirring from time to time until softened. Add the courgettes and aubergine slices and combine well, then stir-fry over a medium high heat for 2–3 minutes until everything begins to colour.

Add the garlic and stir for 1 minute. Add the pepper, the sun-dried tomato paste and the chopped tomatoes, and stir well to combine. Bring to a simmer, cover and turn the heat down low. Cook gently, stirring from time to time, for 45 minutes, or until everything is tender. Stir in most of the basil leaves and cook for 1 further minute.

Ten minutes before the ratatouille is ready, preheat the oven to 180°C/365°F/Gas 4. When the ratatouille is cooked, spoon it into four ovenproof gratin dishes and make a well in the centre of each. Break 1 egg into each well. Put the dishes on a large baking tray and bake in centre of the preheated oven for 15 minutes, or until the egg whites are cooked but the yolks are still runny. Serve hot, garnished with the rest of the basil leaves.

Tips
• To save time or if you don't want to use the oven, you could simply add four lightly poached eggs to the dishes of ratatouille.
• The ratatouille can be used as a tasty side vegetable with chicken, beef, lamb or swordfish steaks. It is great, too, stirred into a robust pasta shape such as quills, to which you could add a sprinkling of Parmesan cheese. Alternatively, serve it with grilled halloumi or feta cheese and some crusty bread. In addition, it turns the following recipe into a hearty supper dish.

POTATO, CHEESE AND RATATOUILLE PIE
Serves 4

Particularly suitable for: families, maintenance dieters, vegetarians
Ideal for: winter, weekend suppers
You will need: a family-sized baking dish, e.g. a lasagne dish

knob butter
1 heaped tablespoon sauce flour
500ml skimmed milk
1 teaspoon Dijon mustard
100g strong Cheddar cheese
4 medium old potatoes (about 800g in total)
cooking oil spray
1 quantity Ratatouille (see Tip)
1 heaped tablespoon grated Parmesan cheese
2 heaped tablespoons wholewheat rough breadcrumbs

Heat the butter in a small non-stick saucepan. When it has

melted, remove from the heat and stir in the sauce flour. Replace on a medium heat and gradually add the skimmed milk, stirring all the time, until you have a smooth pouring sauce. Add the mustard and the Cheddar, and stir again until the cheese is melted and well combined. Remove from the heat.

Peel the potatoes and cut them into rounds about 0.5cm thick. Parboil them for approximately 4 minutes or until they are about two-thirds cooked. Drain carefully.

Preheat the oven to 190°C/375°F/Gas 5. Spray the base of the baking dish with the cooking oil spray. Place a third of the potato slices on the bottom in one layer. Spoon half the ratatouille mixture over the top of the potatoes, spreading it evenly. Cover with another third of the potatoes, and follow with the remainder of the ratatouille. Finish with the remaining third of the potatoes. Pour the cheese sauce over the top, spreading it evenly.

In a small bowl, combine the Parmesan cheese and breadcrumbs, and scatter over the cheese sauce. Bake in the preheated oven for 25 minutes, or until the top is golden and bubbling. Serve hot.

 Tips

• Follow the instructions for making the ratatouille as in the previous recipe, to the point where the basil is added but omitting the eggs.

• Serve with plenty of green vegetables or a large leaf salad.

Desserts

BAKED BANANAS
Serves 4

Particularly suitable for: families, novice cooks, vegetarians
Ideal for: winter or autumn
Used in: Family Plan, Day 2

4 medium bananas
4 tablespoons orange juice
2 tablespoons maple syrup
4 ready-to-eat dried apricots, chopped

Preheat the oven to 190°C/375°F/Gas 5. Place the bananas in their skins on a baking tray and bake in the preheated oven for 15 minutes or until soft all through when pierced. Meanwhile, gently heat the juice, syrup and apricots in a small pan, stirring occasionally.

When the bananas are cooked, serve each on a plate, slit down the inner curve, with the sauce divided evenly and poured into the opening.

 Tips
- The bananas should not be overripe.
- You can use other dried fruit in this dish, such as sultanas. If liked, sprinkle some chopped nuts into the sauce (not suitable for children under five).
- This dish is good served with Greek yoghurt, low-fat bio yoghurt or, for an occasional treat, crème fraiche.
- For adults only, add 1 tablespoon of brandy or orange liqueur to the sauce as it heats.

AUTUMN FRUIT CRUMBLE
Serves 4

Particularly suitable for: maintenance dieters, novice cooks, vegetarians
Ideal for: late summer or autumn, weekends
Used in: Maintenance Plan, Day 1

500g ripe red or golden plums (e.g. Victoria), stoned and halved
200g blackberries and/or raspberries
2 tablespoons brown sugar
half-teaspoon ground cinnamon
1 tablespoon water
1 tablespoon golden syrup
25g butter
100g muesli base (see Tip)
1 heaped tablespoon sunflower seeds
2 heaped tablespoons chopped nuts

Place the plums, berries and half the sugar in a pie dish. Sprinkle with the cinnamon and water, and combine well. Preheat the oven to 190°C/375°F/Gas 5.

In a small saucepan, melt the syrup, butter and remaining sugar over a low heat.

In the meantime, combine in a mixing bowl the muesli, seeds and chopped nuts. When the syrup mixture has melted, pour it over the muesli and stir well to combine. Spread this over the fruit in the pie dish. Bake in the pre-heated oven for 20–25 minutes or until the topping is golden and the fruit is cooked. Serve either hot or warm.

Tips
- You can buy muesli base at any health food shop. Alternatively simply use good-quality rolled oats.
- You can vary the fruit – any ripe soft stone or berry fruit will be fine.
- This goes well with Greek yoghurt or 8 per cent fat natural fromage frais.

BERRY COMPOTE FOOL
Serves 4

Particularly suitable for: maintenance dieters, novice cooks, vegetarians
Ideal for: dinner parties, summer
Used in: Maintenance Plan, Day 2
You will need: a lidded ovenproof dish

500g mixed berries (see Tip)
1 rounded tablespoon sugar
1 tablespoon water
200g Greek yoghurt
200g low-fat natural fromage frais
fresh mint sprigs

Preheat the oven to 180°C/365°F/Gas 4. Place the berries in a lidded ovenproof dish. Sprinkle over the sugar and water, cover and bake in the preheated oven for 15–20 minutes, or until the fruit is tender (but not overcooked) and some juice has been released. Allow to cool.

Reserve 4 dessertspoons of the fruit and set aside.

In a bowl, mix together the Greek yoghurt and fromage frais. Stir in the bulk of the fruit, using a gentle movement to create a marbled effect. Spoon into four individual dessert glasses. Top each with 1 dessertspoonful of the reserved fruit and refrigerate. Serve chilled, garnished with a mint sprig.

 Tips

• To avoid using a great deal of sugar in this recipe, choose mainly berries that are naturally extra-sweet, such as strawberries, blackberries and redcurrants. Add a few sharper berries, such as raspberries or blueberries.

• If you don't want to use the oven, you could poach the fruits with the sugar and water in a saucepan over a very low heat, being careful not to let the fruits disintegrate or overcook.

PINEAPPLE AND PAPAYA KEBABS
Serves 2

Particularly suitable for: novice cooks, slimmers, vegetarians
Ideal for: all year round, dinner parties
You will need: metal skewers or small wooden brochette sticks

---

1 ripe papaya
4 rings fresh pineapple, core removed
1 tablespoon runny honey
juice of 1 lime
knob of butter

If using wooden brochette sticks, soak in water for 1–2 hours to prevent burning under the grill.

Peel and deseed the papaya, and cut the flesh into bite-sized chunks. Cut the pineapple into chunks. In a small non-stick saucepan, warm the honey with the lime juice and butter. Meanwhile, thread the fruit alternately on to the skewers or brochette sticks.

Preheat the grill to high. Place the fruit kebabs on the rack in a grill pan and brush with a little of the sauce. Place the pan under the grill so that the fruit is about 5cm from the heat. Grill, turning once, for 5 minutes, or until the fruit turns slightly brown. Serve hot, with the remaining sauce drizzled over.

 Tips

- If liked, add a dash of rum to the honey and lime sauce, or a little finely chopped stem ginger.
- You can tell whether a papaya is ripe because its skin will have turned orange and the flesh will give slightly to the touch.
- Other fruits can be used (for example, mango or banana chunks), but try to use the pineapple as it offers a lift to the sweetness of the other fruits.
- Greek yoghurt or a little crème fraiche goes well with this.

WINTER FRUIT SALAD
Serves 4

Particularly suitable for: novice cooks, maintenance dieters, vegetarians
Ideal for: winter

---

2 oranges
1 green-skinned apple
2 kiwifruit
75g green seedless grapes
100ml apple juice

If possible, use a chopping board with a deep channel to catch the juices.

Peel the oranges and remove all the pith. Cut into segments and place in a glass serving bowl together with any juice. Core and slice the apple, leaving the skin on, and place in the bowl. Peel and slice the kiwifruit, halve the grapes and add to the bowl. Stir well to combine. Pour over the apple juice. Refrigerate for 1–2 hours. Serve chilled.

 Tips
- This salad is good as a dessert, but is equally useful for breakfast with some bio yoghurt.
- It will keep, covered, for 1–2 days in the fridge.

Drinks

FRUIT AND YOGHURT SMOOTHIE
Serves 2

Particularly suitable for: couples, vegetarians
Ideal for: breakfast, summer
Used in: Couples Plan, Day 1; Maintenance Plan, Day 2
You will need: an electric blender

---

2 ripe peaches
100g fresh raspberries
200ml low-fat natural bio yoghurt
1 tablespoon runny honey
50ml peach juice

Peel and stone the peaches, chop them and place in an electric blender with any juice that runs off. Add the raspberries, yoghurt, honey and peach juice. Blend for a few seconds until you have a smooth drink. Refrigerate. Pour into two glasses and serve chilled.

 Tips
- You can use nectarines instead of peaches.
- If you can't find peach juice, use mango juice instead.

BANANA AND STRAWBERRY SMOOTHIE
Serves 2

Particularly suitable for: couples, vegetarians
Ideal for: breakfast, summer
You will need: an electric blender

125g strawberries
1 large or 2 small just ripe bananas
300ml skimmed milk

Hull and chop the strawberries, and place in the electric blender. Peel the bananas, roughly chop them and add to the blender, together with the milk. Blend for a few seconds until you have a smooth drink. Refrigerate. Pour into two glasses and serve chilled.

 Tips
- If the bananas are underripe they won't purée very well – but if they are too ripe they become oversweet.
- In winter, you can use an orange, peeled and segmented, with the pith removed, instead of the strawberries.

6 FOOD REFERENCE CHARTS

This section is a back-up to the Traffic Light food lists that appear in Chapter 2 and also provides more detailed information for committed users.

All you need to follow the Traffic Light Diet is the simple lists of GREEN, AMBER and RED foods that appear on pages 29–43 (and again as a tear-out at the end of the book). However, you may want a little more detailed information about portion sizes or the nutritional benefits – or otherwise – of a particular food, or you may want to look up a food to see whether it is GREEN, AMBER or RED.

These food reference charts list over 400 foods alphabetically, making it quick and easy to find a food.

Example 1: You want to eat a boiled egg. You look up 'Dairy Produce and Eggs', and scan down this alphabetical list until you come to 'eggs'. Scan further until you find 'boiled'. You will find that boiled eggs are AMBER, and the notes will tell you that you can eat up to six eggs a week; also that a small portion is one medium egg and a medium portion is two medium eggs.

Example 2: You want to eat some brown rice. You look up 'Grains' and scan down to find 'rice'. Scan down here until you find 'brown, basmati'. You will find that brown basmati rice is AMBER and the notes will tell you that a medium portion is 75g dry weight.

All portion sizes given are as a guide only. You will

remember that on the Traffic Light Diet there is no need to weigh food portions; just use your common sense as to what is a small or medium portion.

Further information on how many of the AMBER and RED foods you should eat a day appears in Questions 7 to 11 in Chapter 4 and within the basic listings on pages 29–43.

For your reference, foods are listed in these charts under the following alphabetical categories:

Breads
Cakes, Biscuits and Baked Goods
Confectionery and Sweeteners
Dairy Produce and Eggs
Desserts and Ices
Drinks
Fats and Oils
Fish and Seafood
Fruit
Grains and Cereals
Nuts and Seeds
Meat and Poultry
Pastry and Pies
Ready Meals and Takeaways
Sauces, Dressings and Condiments
Snacks
Soups
Vegetables
Vegetarian Proteins and Pulses

PRODUCT	TRAFFIC LIGHT COLOUR	NOTES
BREADS Brown bread	AMBER	Slightly higher in vitamins, minerals and fibre than white bread. An average portion is 2 small slices.
Flatbreads: chapati	AMBER	Moderate in fat. An average portion is half a chapati.
naan	RED	High in fat. A small portion is a quarter of a naan.
wrap	AMBER	Moderate to low in fat. An average portion is one wrap.
Garlic bread	RED	Very high in fat and saturates. A small portion is a 5cm slice.
Granary bread	AMBER	Similar to brown in content. An average portion is two small slices.
Oatbread	AMBER	Higher in soluble fibre than wheat breads and lower on the glycaemic index. An average portion is two small slices.
Pitta bread: white	AMBER	Fairly low in fat but may be high in salt.
wholewheat	AMBER	Higher in fibre than white pitta. An average portion is one pitta.
Rye bread	AMBER	Lower on the glycaemic index

		than wheat bread. An average portion is two small slices.
White bread	AMBER	May be high in salt. Low in fibre. In the UK contains added calcium. Best to choose wholemeal, rye or oat bread at least some of the time. An average portion is two small slices.
Wholewheat bread	AMBER	Good fibre and nutrient content, fairly low in fat. An average portion is two small slices.

CAKES, BISCUITS AND BAKED GOODS

Cakes, all	RED	All cakes are high in calories and most are high in fat and/or sugar and sometimes artificial additives. Rich fruit cakes are some of the most nutritious. A small portion is a 50g slice.
Biscuits, cookies and bars, sweet, all	RED	All sweet biscuits are relatively high in calories, fat and/or sugar. A small portion is one biscuit.
Biscuits for cheese etc., savoury or semi-sweet	RED	Usually high in fat and salt and/ or sugar. Cream crackers and water biscuits are included here. A small portion is one large or two small biscuits.
oatcakes	AMBER	Choose low-sugar, low-salt varieties of oatcake. Oats are a good source of soluble fibre An average portion is two oatcakes.

Rice cakes:		
brown	AMBER	Low in fat and containing some fibre. An average portion is two rice cakes.
white	RED	White rice cakes are a low-fat food but contain little goodness or fibre. A small portion is one rice cake.
Rye crispbreads	AMBER	Low in fat and high in nutrients and fibre. An average portion is two crispbreads.
Cereal bars	RED	Usually high in fat and sugar and sometimes salt. A small portion is one bar.
Croissant	RED	Very high in saturated fat and calories. A small portion is one mini croissant.
Scones and teacakes	RED	Lower in fat and sugar than most cakes but still high in calories and contain little nutritional benefits. Can encourage fluid retention due to high refined carbohydrate content. A small portion is one small scone or teacake.

CONFECTIONERY AND SWEETENERS

Chocolate:		
dark	RED	While high in fat and sugar, dark chocolate contains polyphenols, which may be good for health. A small

		portion is 30g, or one very small bar, or two chocolates.
milk	RED	Contains few polyphenols.
white	RED	Contains no polyphenols.
Honey	RED	Fewer calories than sugar but less sweet. Good-quality honey contains a few vitamins and minerals and has a mild antibiotic action. A small portion is 1–2 teaspoons.
Sugar, all	RED	Contains calories but no other nutrients. High on the glycaemic index. A small portion is 1 teaspoon.
Sweets, all	RED (!!!)	Best avoided as most sweets contain no nutritional benefits and are high in sugar and artificial additives

DAIRY PRODUCE AND EGGS

Cheese

blue	RED	High in saturates, calories, salt. A small portion is a matchbox-sized piece.
Brie, Camembert	AMBER	Medium high in fat, calories, salt. An average portion is a wrapped triangle or a piece 1.5 times the size of a matchbox.
Cheddar	RED	As blue cheese.
Cheddar, half-fat	AMBER	Medium high in fat, calories

		and salt. An average portion is a piece 1.5 times the size of a matchbox.
cottage	AMBER	Low in fat and calories, usually high in salt. An average portion is 2 tablespoons.
cream cheese	RED	High in saturates, calories and fairly high in salt. A small portion is 1 rounded tablespoon.
Edam	RED	As blue cheese.
feta	AMBER	As half-fat Cheddar.
goat's cheese, soft	AMBER	As Brie and Camembert.
mascarpone	RED	As cream cheese.
mozzarella, Italian	AMBER	As Brie and Camembert.
Parmesan/ Pecorino	RED	High in saturates, calories and salt but with a very strong flavour so a little goes a long way. A small portion is a matchbox-sized piece or 1 rounded tablespoonful of shaved or grated Parmesan.
soft cheese, low-fat	AMBER	Medium to low in fat and calories usually high in salt. A medium portion is 1–2 level tablespoons.
Cheese dip: low-fat	AMBER	Low in fat and calories, usually high in salt. A medium portion is 2 tablespoons.

full-fat	RED	High in fat, calories and salt. A small portion is 1 level table-spoon.

Cream

aerosol	RED	Mostly air, so is low in calories per 'squirt'. A small portion is two squirts.
crème fraiche/sour	RED	Medium to high in fat. A small portion is 1 tablespoon.
double	RED	High in fat. A small portion is 1 level tablespoon.
half-fat	RED	Medium in fat. A small portion is 2 tablespoons.
single	RED	Medium to high in fat. A small portion is 2 tablespoons.
whipping	RED	As crème fraiche.

Eggs

boiled or poached	AMBER	A nutritious protein source, medium fat. An average portion is 1–2 medium eggs.
duck eggs	AMBER	As hen's eggs.
fried	RED	Medium to high in fat. A small portion is one small fried egg.
quail's eggs	AMBER	An average portion is four eggs.
scrambled: with butter and cream	RED	High in calories, fat and choles-terol. A small portion is 1 table-spoon.

with skimmed milk in non-stick pan	AMBER	An average portion is two medium eggs.
scotch	RED	The meat coating is high in fat and calories. A small portion is half a Scotch egg.
Fromage frais:		
0% fat natural	GREEN	High in protein, low in fat, low in calories.
8% fat natural	AMBER	High protein, medium fat. An average portion is 100ml.
fruit, all kinds	RED	May contain a lot of sugar and/or artificial additives. A small portion is a 60ml pot.
Milk		
goat's milk	RED	Similar protein and fat content to cow's whole milk. A small portion is 100ml.
semi-skimmed	AMBER	A useful source of nutrients including calcium. A medium portion is 200ml.
skimmed	GREEN	A good source of calcium, protein, some B vits.
soya milk	GREEN	Buy the calcium-enriched, unsweetened variety.
Whole (full-fat) milk	RED	Full-fat cow's milk is quite high in fat and calories. A small portion is 100ml.

Yoghurt		
fruit, all kinds	RED	Usually high in sugar and/or additives. A small portion is one individual 125ml pot.
Greek, full-fat	RED	Fairly high in fat so have moderate portions only – a little goes a long way. A portion is 100ml.
Greek, half-fat	AMBER	Lower in calories than full-fat Greek but may contain bulking agents. An average portion is 125ml.
natural/bio, whole milk	AMBER	Can help settle the digestive system. Medium in fat. An average portion is 125ml.
natural/bio, low-fat	GREEN	An excellent food for protein, calcium and B vits. Can help colonise the gut with friendly bacteria.

DESSERTS AND ICES

Custard: full-fat	RED	High in fat, sugar and calories. A small portion is one individual tub.
low-fat	RED	Lower in fat and calories. A small portion is 100ml. A reasonable source of calcium.
Cheesecake	RED	High in fat, sugar and calories. A small portion is 100g.

Crème caramel	RED	High in fat, sugar and calories. A small portion is one individual dessert.
Ice cream, vanilla	RED	High in fat and sugar; often made using trans fats. A small portion is 100ml or one individual tub.
Ice lolly	RED	Contains no fat and quite low in calories, but high in sugar and additives. A home-made lolly using fruit juice is a little better. A small portion is one individual lolly.
Jelly	RED	Fat-free but can be quite high in sugar and packet jellies are high in artificial additives. Sugar-free jelly is low in calories. A small portion is one individual tub.
Mousse, chocolate	RED	High in fat, sugar and calories. A small portion is one individual dessert. Calories vary a great deal from brand to brand – try to find those under 150 calories a pot.
Meringue	RED	Although virtually fat-free, meringues are high in sugar and can encourage a sweet tooth. However, they can make a good occasional dessert with fresh fruit. A small portion is one individual meringue.
Rice pudding	RED	Reasonable source of calcium but high in calories. A small

		portion is one individual tub or 3 tablespoons.
Sponge pudding	RED	High in sugar and calories; quite high in fat. A small portion is 150g.
Trifle, fruit	RED	High in sugar, fat and calories. A small portion is one individual tub.

DRINKS

Alcoholic: beer and lager	RED	Small amounts of darker beers are generally good for health; high in anti-oxidants. A small portion is a half-pint.
spirits	RED	Darker spirits such as dark rum and whisky contain useful amounts of anti-oxidants. A small portion is a double measure.
wine	RED	Small amounts of wine, particularly red wine, are a good source of polyphenol anti-oxidants. A small portion is one small wineglass.
Coffee	AMBER	Two cups a day. Avoid with meals. Avoid if pregnant.
Fruit juices, all	RED	Contain a lot of sugar, quite high in calories and fruit acids. Cause quick rise in blood sugar. A small portion is 100ml (one small wineglass).

Fruit smoothies, all	AMBER	Quite high in calories but most contain good amounts of vitamins, fibre and phytochemicals. An average portion is 250ml (one medium glass).
Milk – see Dairy Produce		
Milk drinks, hot e.g. malted, hot chocolate	RED	Can be high in fat, sugar and calories. Reasonable source of calcium. Choose low-fat, reduced-sugar brands if possible. A small portion is 150ml (one average cup).
Soda water	AMBER	Can be used occasionally as a spritzer mixer. Calorie-free but contains sodium.
Soft drinks e.g. cola, orangeade, squash	RED (!!!)	Contain a lot of sugar and calories as well as additives and acid. A small portion is one small bottle or can. Best avoided.
Soft drinks, low-calorie	RED (!!!)	Artificial sweeteners don't wean you away from a sweet tooth; most of these drinks contain a lot of artificial additives and acid. A small portion is one small bottle or can. Best avoided.

Tea:		
black/Indian	AMBER	Contains caffeine so should be limited to a few cups a day, which are enough to produce benefits from the polyphenols that it contains.
green	AMBER	As black tea.
camomile	GREEN	Relaxing caffeine-free herbal tea.
lemon balm	GREEN	As camomile.
Oolong	AMBER	As black tea.
peppermint	GREEN	Energising caffeine-free tea, good for digestive upsets.
redbush	GREEN	Caffeine-free tea similar in taste to standard tea. High in anti-oxidants.
white	AMBER	As black tea.
Tomato juice	GREEN	Very low in sugars and calories compared to most other juices. Rich in carotenoids.
Vegetable juice, commercial, made from several different vegetables	GREEN	Vegetable juices are much lower in sugar and calorie than fruit juices and contain less acid. Rich in carotenoids and vitamins.
Waters, flavoured, carbonated	RED	Both diet and non-diet versions are little better than colas, containing a range of additives and artificial sweeteners. A small portion is one small bottle or can.

Water	GREEN	Drink approximately 1.5 litres a day for good health. Adequate water helps prevent dehydration, dry skin and constipation. However, drinking a great deal of water at one time (e.g. more than 2 litres) is dangerous as it dilutes the body salts too much.

FATS AND OILS

Butter	RED	High in saturated fat but preferable to hard margarines (these may be high in trans fats, which are probably worse for health than saturated fat). A small portion is 1 teaspoon.
Cooking oil spray	AMBER	Use several sprays to coat pans before cooking.
Dripping, lard, suet	RED	High in saturated fat and calories. Best avoided.
Groundnut (peanut) oil	AMBER	A fairly high mono-unsaturated oil; can be used occasionally instead of olive oil in cooking. An average portion is 1 tablespoon.
Low-fat spread	RED	Moderately high in fat and may contain trans fats. A small portion is 1 teaspoon.
Olive oil	AMBER	High in mono-unsaturates; heart protective. Good for both cooking and using cold. An

		average portion is 1 tablespoon.
Vegetable and seed oil: blended	RED	Cheaper blends of vegetable oils are high in the type of polyunsaturated fat that we should limit in the diet, especially in cooking as it oxidises easily. A small portion is 1–2 teaspoons.
corn oil	RED	As blended vegetable oil.
rapeseed oil	AMBER	As groundnut oil.
safflower oil	RED	As blended vegetable oil.
sesame seed oil	AMBER	As groundnut oil.
sunflower oil	RED	As blended vegetable oil.
walnut oil	AMBER	High in omega-3 essential fats. Makes a good alternative to olive oil for salads etc. Not suitable for cooking. An average portion is 1 tablespoon.

FISH AND SEAFOOD

Battered and/or deep-fried fish	RED	Very high in fat and calories. A small portion is 125g.
Cod	GREEN	Low in fat and high in protein. You can eat a large portion of white fish several times a week.
Crab: fresh or frozen	GREEN	Low-fat, high-protein seafood. Best eaten fresh in summer.

canned in brine	RED	High in salt. A small portion is one 60g can.
Eel	AMBER	Oily fish high in omega-3s (see page 99 and Appendix for restrictions); a medium portion is 140g.
Haddock	GREEN	As cod.
Hake	GREEN	As cod.
Halibut	GREEN	As cod.
Herring	AMBER	Oily fish (see page 99 and Appendix for restrictions); a medium portion is 140g.
Kipper	RED	Smoked fish may be carcinogenic so eat infrequently. A small portion is one small kipper fillet.
Lobster	AMBER	Low in fat and calories and high in protein but has fairly high cholesterol levels. A medium portion (shelled weight) is 100g.
Mackerel: fresh	AMBER	As herring.
canned in tomato sauce	AMBER	High in lycopene as well as omega-3s. A medium portion is one 100g can.
Marlin	AMBER	Pregnant women, women intending to become pregnant and children under 16 should avoid marlin (see page 99 and Appendix for restrictions on certain fish). A medium portion is 140g.

Monkfish	GREEN	As cod.
Mullet	GREEN	As cod.
Mussels	GREEN	Low in fat and high in protein. In season from September to April.
Octopus	AMBER	Low in fat and high in protein, fairly high in cholesterol. A medium portion is 140g.
Oysters	GREEN	As mussels – in season from September to April.
Pilchards in tomato sauce	AMBER	As mackerel in tomato sauce.
Plaice	GREEN	As cod.
Prawns: fresh or frozen	AMBER	A low-fat, high-protein food but high in cholesterol. A medium portion (shelled weight) is 100g.
canned in brine	RED	High in salt. A small portion is 50g.
Salmon: fresh or frozen	AMBER	As herring.
canned in oil	RED	Very high in fat, with reduced omega-3s. A small portion is 100g.
canned in brine	RED	High in salt, with reduced omega-3s. A small portion is 100g.
smoked	RED	As kippers but a small portion is 50g/two average slices.

Sardines:
  fresh
  canned in
  tomato
  sauce
	AMBER
	AMBER
		As herring.
		As mackerel in tomato sauce.

Scallops	GREEN	As crab.
Sea bass	GREEN	As cod.
Sea bream	GREEN	As cod.
Shark	AMBER	As marlin.
Skate	GREEN	As cod.
Snapper	GREEN	As cod.
Sole	GREEN	As cod.
Squid	AMBER	As octopus.
Swordfish	AMBER	As marlin.
Taramasalata	RED	A fish paste/dip made from cod's roes. Very high in fat and salt. A small portion is 1 tablespoon.
Trout, sea or river	AMBER	As herring.

Tuna:
  fresh
  canned in oil
 	
  canned in
  water
	AMBER
	RED
	
	GREEN
		As herring.
		Very high in fat and loses most of its omega-3s. A small portion is one 100g can.
		As cod, but if you are pregnant or intending to become pregnant, have no more than four medium cans a week.

canned in brine	RED	High in salt, low in omega-3s. A small portion is one 100g can.
Turbot	GREEN	As cod.
Whitebait, sprats, deep fried	RED	Very high in fat and calories. A small portion is 100g.
Whiting	GREEN	As cod.

FRUIT

Apples:		
dessert	GREEN	Can help lower cholesterol and asthma. Eat as fresh as you can for more vitamin C content. A low glycaemic index food.
cooking	GREEN	Add cinnamon and dried fruit to cooking apples to reduce the need for added sugar.
dried	AMBER	A medium portion is three or four dried apple rings.
pie	RED	See pies and pastries.
Apricots:		
dried ready-to-eat	AMBER	Rich in iron, potassium and carotenoids. A medium portion is four or five pieces. A low glycaemic index food.
fresh	GREEN	A low glycaemic index food that can help keep hunger at bay.
Avocado – see Vegetables		
Bananas: fresh, small	GREEN	A very good source of potassium.

dried banana chips	RED	One of the few starchy fruits, higher in calories than most. High on the glycaemic index. High in calories and sugar; best kept for an occasional snack. A small portion is five banana chips.
Blackberries	GREEN	Unlike most fruits, they contain good amounts of vitamin E. Also high in vitamin C and cancer-fighting ellagic acid.
Blackcurrants	GREEN	Very rich in vitamin C – just 50g fruit contains more than the recommended daily amount for adults. Also high in anti-oxidants, including lutein.
Blueberries	GREEN	The top-ranked food on the ORAC scale, which measures anti-oxidant activity, thus very good for anti-ageing, brainpower and healthy skin. Regular consumption can reduce levels of LDL cholesterol.
Cherries	GREEN	High in ellagic acid and other polyphenols, some of which are lost if cooked. Low on the glycaemic index so a good snack food for warding off hunger.
Cranberries: fresh	GREEN	Can help urinary tract infections; high in anti-bacterial polyphenols. A very high intake can cause diarrhoea; maximum beneficial intake may be 500ml a day.

dried	AMBER	A medium portion is 1 heaped tablespoon.
Currants, dried	AMBER	High in potassium. A medium portion is one handful.
Damsons	GREEN	High in potassium and carotenoids.
Dates: dried	AMBER	High in sugar but also very high in potassium and a good source of calcium and iron. A medium portion is three or four dates.
fresh	GREEN	Quite high in sugar and calories but a good source of many nutrients, including folate and potassium.
Figs: dried	AMBER	High in sugar but also very high in fibre, potassium, calcium, magnesium and iron. A medium portion is two dried figs.
fresh	GREEN	A good source of potassium, calcium and carotenoids. Contains the laxative compound mucin.
Gooseberries	GREEN	Contain good amounts of vitamins C and E, and carotenoids.
Grapefruit	GREEN	High in vitamin C; the pink variety contains carotenoids. Low on the glycaemic index so a good food for breakfast, for preventing mid-morning hunger.

Grapes	GREEN	Higher in sugar and calories than many fruits but a good source of potassium. Red and black varieties contain high levels of ellagic acid and other polyphenols to help prevent disease.
Greengages	GREEN	Low on the glycaemic index, making them a good between-meal snack
Kiwifruit	GREEN	A very good source of vitamin C – one fruit contains approximately an adult's entire daily recommended amount.
Kumquats	GREEN	Citrus fruits, which can be eaten whole. As the pith and peel contain anti-oxidant plant chemicals as well as the flesh, they provide a very good amount of anti-oxidant plant chemicals. When eaten whole, also very high in fibre.
Lemons	GREEN	A good source of vitamin C and the plant chemical limonene, which has an anti-cancer effect and can lower levels of LDL cholesterol.
Limes	GREEN	As lemons.
Loganberries	GREEN	A good source of potassium, calcium and folate.
Lychees	GREEN	A good source of vitamin C and fibre.

Mandarins	GREEN	A good source of vitamin C, calcium and carotenoids.
Mango	GREEN	High in vitamins C and E, calcium, and other vitamins and minerals. Its high levels of carotenoids may protect against cancers.
Melon	GREEN	Orange-fleshed varieties, such as cantaloupe, are high in carotenoids and also contain more vitamin C and calcium than pale-fleshed varieties.
Nectarines	GREEN	High in vitamin C and carotenoids.
Olives: fresh	GREEN	Olives contain flavonoids for heart health and are rich in fibre and vitamin E.
in oil	AMBER	High in calories. A medium portion is six olives.
in brine	RED	Very high in salt and should be avoided or well rinsed. A small portion is three or four olives.
Oranges	GREEN	High in vitamin C, fibre, potassium, folate, calcium. Blood oranges contain more carotenoids.
Papaya (pawpaw)	GREEN	High in vitamin C, carotenoids and soluble fibre for heart health. Contains enzymes that help to digest protein foods.

Passion fruit	GREEN	High in vitamin C and carotenoids.
Peaches: fresh dried	GREEN AMBER	High in vitamin C and carotenoids. White-fleshed peaches contain little carotene. As dried apricots.
Pears	GREEN	A good source of fibre; low on the glycaemic index so good for a between-meal snack.
Pineapple	GREEN	Raw pineapple contains the plant enzyme bromelain, which can aid digestion. Other chemicals may be anti-cancer. Is high in acid so best eaten with a meal to avoid tooth decay.
Plums	GREEN	High in potassium and carotenoids and low on the glycaemic index, making them a good between-meal snack.
Prunes	AMBER	Dried plums, which are high in fibre and have a natural laxative effect. Very high in potassium and iron, and a good source of calcium. A medium portion is four dried, ready-to-eat prunes.
Raisins	AMBER	Very high in calories and sugars but an excellent source of potassium and iron. A medium portion is one small handful.
Raspberries	GREEN	An excellent source of vitamin

		C, fibre and folate with good amounts of potassium and calcium. A good source of ellagic acid (see cherries).
Rhubarb	AMBER	Eat in moderate amounts because the high levels of oxalates that it contains inhibit the absorption of minerals. Avoid if you have kidney stones. High intakes of oxalate-rich foods can be toxic. Has a laxative effect. A medium portion is two sticks.
Satsumas	GREEN	See Mandarins.
Star fruit	GREEN	A good source of vitamin C.
Strawberries	GREEN	A very good source of vitamin C and ellagic acid.
Sultanas	AMBER	High in calories and sugar but a good source of potassium and iron. A medium portion is one small handful.
Tangerines	GREEN	See Mandarins.

GRAINS AND CEREALS

Breakfast cereals		
All Bran	AMBER	Very high in fibre; high in many vitamins and minerals, low in fat and calories. Has a low glycaemic index, contains sugar and is high in salt. A medium portion is 5 tablespoons.

Bran Flakes	AMBER	Contains sugar and is high in salt. Low in fat, a reasonable source of fibre. A medium portion is 5 tablespoons.
Breakfast biscuits (e.g. Weetabix)	AMBER	Wheat biscuits are low in sugar with a reasonable amount of fibre and a range of vitamins and minerals. A medium portion is two biscuits.
Cheerios	AMBER	Moderately high in sugar; high in salt, moderate in fibre, a good source of calcium. A medium portion is 5 tablespoons.
Chocolate-coated cereals	RED	Higher in fat, sugar and calories than plain cereals. A small portion is 3 tablespoons.
Caramel-coated cereals	RED	High in sugar and calories. A small portion is 3 tablespoons.
Clusters	RED	Crunchy cereals that have been baked into crisp clusters are usually higher in fat and sugar than plainly cooked cereals. A small portion is 3 tablespoons.
Coco Pops	RED	High in sugar, moderately high in salt. Contains little fibre but a range of added vitamins/minerals. A small portion is 3 tablespoons.
Cornflakes	RED	Fairly low in sugar but very high

		in salt; also low in fibre. A small portion is 3 tablespoons.
Frosties	RED	As Coco Pops.
Fruit 'n' Fibre	AMBER	Moderately high in sugar and salt but low in fat; contains good amounts of fibre, vitamins and minerals. A medium portion is 5 tablespoons.
Muesli, no added-sugar variety	AMBER	Muesli can contain various grains, including oats and wheat. Look for high-oat varieties, which contain good amounts of soluble fibre for heart health. Muesli has a good fibre content and, if it is high in nuts and seeds, should contain good amounts of essential fats and vitamin E. If it is high in dried fruits, it should contain good amounts of iron and potassium. A medium portion is 4 tablespoons.
Oat cereal, instant	AMBER	Instant cereals (to mix with boiling water) are low in sugar and salt, have moderate fibre and are high in calcium but compared with traditional oat breakfasts are higher on the glycaemic index. A medium portion is 250ml.
Porridge	AMBER	High in soluble fibre and, if made with water and/or skimmed milk, low in calories and fat; low on the

		glycaemic index. A medium portion is 300ml.
Puffed Wheat	AMBER	Low in sugar, salt and calories. A good source of fibre, some vitamins and minerals. A medium portion is 5 tablespoons.
Ricicles	RED	High in sugar, low in fibre, moderate in salt. A small portion is 3 tablespoons.
Rice Krispies	RED	Low in sugar but also low in fibre, moderately high in salt, with added vitamins and minerals. A small portion is 3 tablespoons.
Shredded Wheat	AMBER	High-fibre wholegrain cereal, low in sugar and salt and containing a good range of vitamins and minerals. A medium portion is two Shredded Wheat.
Sugar Puffs	RED	Low in salt but very high in sugar and low in fibre. A small portion is 3 tablespoons.

Grains

Barley:		
pot	AMBER	A low-fat, high-fibre source of iron and other minerals and the vitamin B group. A medium portion is 75g (uncooked weight).
pearl	RED	Has had the fibre and vitamins stripped from it. A small portion is 45g (uncooked weight).

Bulghur wheat	AMBER	A good source of iron, B vitamins and fibre. A medium portion is 75g (uncooked weight).
Couscous: instant	RED	Pre-cooked semolina with few nutrients remaining. A small portion is 45g (unreconstituted weight).
traditional	AMBER	Contains good amounts of fibre, vitamins and minerals. A medium portion is 75g (uncooked weight).
Noodles: rice	RED	Highly refined rice pasta. A small portion is 45g (uncooked weight).
egg thread	RED	High on the glycaemic index. A small portion is 45g (uncooked weight).
Oats: traditional rolled	AMBER	A good source of fibre and soluble fibre, fairly low on the glycaemic index, ideal to help prevent hunger. A medium portion is 50g (uncooked weight).
Pasta: white	RED	Can cause bloating; higher on the glycaemic index than whole-wheat pasta. Contains few vita-mins or minerals and is low in fibre. A small portion is 45g (uncooked weight).
wholewheat	AMBER	Moderately low on the glycaemic

		index. Contains good amounts of vitamin B group and magnesium; has a high fibre content. A medium portion is 75g (uncooked weight).
Polenta	RED	This is cooked using a lot of fat and salt. A small portion is 125g (cooked weight).
Quinoa	AMBER	Not a real grain but classed as such. Rich in iron, folate, magnesium and protein. A medium portion is 75g (uncooked weight).

Rice:
  brown
  basmati
	AMBER	Rich in fibre and B vitamins. Has a low glycaemic index compared with other rices. A medium portion is 75g (uncooked weight). Superior flavour.

white basmati	AMBER	Contains less fibre and vitamins than brown basmati but is also low on the glycaemic index compared with other rices. A medium portion is 75g (uncooked weight) Superior flavour.
all other rices	RED	High on the glycaemic index – best to choose basmati. A small portion is 45g (uncooked weight).

NUTS AND SEEDS

Nuts

Almonds, fresh	AMBER	High in fibre, vitamin E, essential fats, and a range of minerals. A medium portion is six nuts.
Brazils	AMBER	High in selenium for heart health and cancer protection; also contains a range of other minerals. A medium portion is three whole nuts.
Cashews	AMBER	High in iron and zinc, B vitamins and a range of other minerals. High in mono-unsaturated fats. A medium portion is a small handful.
Chestnuts	AMBER	High in potassium and lower in fat than most nuts. A medium portion is eight whole nuts.
Coconut, fresh creamed	RED	Coconut is high in a form of saturated fat. Best used in small amounts. A small portion is one 4cm square of fresh coconut or 1 level tablespoon of creamed coconut or 2 tablespoons of coconut milk, unskimmed.
Hazelnuts	AMBER	Very rich in vitamin E and mono-unsaturates, and high in fibre. A medium portion is a small handful.
Macadamia nuts	AMBER	Very high in mono-unsaturates; also contain magnesium. A medium portion is six nuts.
Peanuts	AMBER	High in vitamin E, protein and

		fibre. Shown to lower levels of LDL cholesterol – as can most fresh nuts. A medium portion is a small handful.
Peanut butter	RED	Very high in fat and calories (although a good source of vitamin E). Try to find the sugar-free variety. A small portion is 1 level dessertspoon.
Pecans	AMBER	High in a range of vitamins and minerals. A medium portion is six pecan halves.
Pistachios	AMBER	A good source of calcium, iron and zinc. A medium portion is a small handful.
Salted/roasted nuts, all kinds	RED	High in salt – and the cooking process destroys much of the B vitamins and essential fats. A small portion is 1 dessertspoon.
Walnuts	AMBER	A good source of folate and a range of other vitamins and minerals. A medium portion is six walnut halves.
Seeds Flaxseeds (linseeds)	AMBER	High in essential omega-3 fats and minerals. Contain lignans, which can help symptoms of the menopause. A medium portion is l dessertspoon.

Pine kernels, fresh	AMBER	High in essential fats, vitamin E and minerals. A medium portion is 1 tablespoon.
Pumpkin seeds, fresh	AMBER	High in essential fats and minerals. A medium portion is 1 tablespoon.
Salted/roasted seeds, all kinds	RED	High in salt; also the cooking process destroys essential fats.
Sunflower seeds, fresh	AMBER	High in essential fats, vitamin E and minerals. A medium portion is 1 tablespoon.
Tahini (sesame seed paste)	RED	Very high in fat and calories but contains a good range of vitamins and minerals. Use in small quantities. A small portion is 1 level dessertspoon.

MEAT AND POULTRY

Meat Bacon, all types	RED	Bacon is high in salt and is often high in fat, calories and saturated fat. If you are going to have a small portion of bacon from time to time, choose the extra-lean, reduced-salt varieties. A small portion of bacon is one standard rasher or two thin extra-lean rashers.
Beef: minced, extra-lean	AMBER	Go for less than 10 per cent fat mince or choose lean braising

		steak at the butchers and get it minced. A medium portion of minced beef is 150g cooked weight.
minced, average	RED	High in fat, calories and saturates. A small portion is 100g cooked weight.
roast, lean	AMBER	If you cut off the fat before eating, roast beef isn't particularly high in fat; only 40 per cent of the fat is saturated. A medium portion is 150g cooked weight or three average slices.
steak, lean	AMBER	If you cut off the fat band before eating, it is fairly low in fat. A medium portion is one 200g steak, cooked weight.
beefburger, lean	AMBER	A good-quality burger made from extra-lean mince is not high in fat. A medium portion is one quarterpounder.
beefburger, other	RED	Can be high in fat and mechanically recovered meat. Best to always choose good-quality lean burgers. A small portion is one small beefburger – around 50g.
beef, corned	RED	High in salt, fat and nitrites. A small portion is 50g or two slices.
Black pudding	RED	Although it is very high in iron, it is also high in fat and salt. A

		small portion is two round slices from a small sausage, dry-fried.
Ham, lean, reduced-salt	AMBER	Most ham is as high in salt as bacon, so should be regarded as RED. If you can find reduced-salt ham, it is a lean, low-calorie source of protein. A medium portion is 75g or three small slices.
Lamb: chop	RED	High in fat. A small portion is one chop.
leg, lean, roast	AMBER	Although higher in fat and calories than lean beef, lamb is a healthy source of protein, B vitamins, iron and zinc. A medium portion is 100g or two average slices.
lamb steak	AMBER	As leg, lean, roast.
fillet	AMBER	From the neck or leg – see leg, lean, roast.
shoulder	RED	Much higher in fat than leg or fillet of lamb, so much higher in calories. If using, cook thoroughly so that more of the fat runs out. A small portion is 80g or two small slices.
Meat pâté	RED	Very high in fat and calories, and often high in salt. A small portion is 1 tablespoon.
Meat pies – see Pastry and Pies		

Offal, including liver and kidneys	AMBER	Low in fat and calories but high in cholesterol. Liver should be avoided by pregnant women because of its very high vitamin A content, which is toxic. Offal is rich in B vitamins and many minerals. A portion is 140g.
Pork: chop	RED	High in fat and calories. A small portion is one small chop.
steak	AMBER	Low in fat and calories. A medium portion is one average steak.
leg, roast	AMBER	If you eat the lean leg only, this is a low-fat roast. Pork is high in B vitamins, zinc and selenium. A medium portion is 100g or two average slices.
fillet	AMBER	As leg.
crackling	RED	Very high in fat. A small portion is one 4cm square.
Rabbit, fillet	AMBER	A low-fat meat containing B vitamins and selenium. A medium portion is 150g meat (weight without bone).
Salami and other deli meats	RED	Most delicatessen meats are very high in fat and salt. A small portion is two thin round slices.
Sausages, standard	RED	Most sausages are very high in fat and salt and most contain artificial additives and nitrites. A small portion is one average sausage. Cook well to disperse more fat.

Veal	AMBER	Low in fat and containing a good range of B vitamins and zinc. A medium portion is one veal escallope.
Venison	AMBER	Low in fat and containing B vitamins, iron and zinc. A medium portion is 150g.

Poultry and game birds

Chicken:

all lean meat	AMBER	Chicken meat, both white and dark, is a low-fat source of protein, containing B vitamins, zinc and selenium. A medium portion is 150g or one average breast or leg.
skin	RED	If you eat the skin on chicken, it becomes higher in fat than lean beef, so remove the skin before eating.

Duck:

lean meat	AMBER	The flesh of duck is quite lean, so if you remove all the fat, you have a healthy source of protein. Duck is mostly mono-unsaturated fat anyway. A good source of iron, selenium and zinc. A medium portion is one duck breast fillet.
fat and skin	RED	Although the fat is mostly mono-unsaturated and therefore not unhealthy, it is very high in calories so should be limited. A

		small portion of crispy duck skin is a piece 3cm square.
Guinea fowl	AMBER	A source of low-fat protein. A medium portion is one guinea fowl breast.
Pheasant	AMBER	Although higher in fat than chicken, it is still a healthy source of protein, and is rich in iron and B vitamins. A medium portion is one average pheasant breast.
Pigeon	AMBER	A low-fat source of protein, containing B vitamins and iron. A medium portion is one pigeon.
Turkey: all lean meat	AMBER	A very low-fat meat, containing good amounts of B vitamins and selenium. The dark meat has much more iron and zinc than the light meat. A medium portion is 150g turkey or three average slices.

PASTRY AND PIES

Danish pastries, all	RED	Very high in calories, sugar and fat. Avoid large Danish pastries. A mini pastry counts as two small portions.
Fruit pies and flans	RED	High in fat, calories and sugar. A small portion is a 100g slice.
Meat pies and pasties	RED	High in fat, saturated fat and calories. A small portion is a 100g slice.

Pastry:		
all types except filo	RED	High in fat, saturated fat and calories. A small portion is a 50g serving.
filo	RED	Lower in fat and calories than other pastry. Can be used for layered pastry desserts and pies with the last layer brushed with olive oil. A small portion is two filo sheets.
Pork pie	RED	High in fat, saturated fat and calories. A small portion is one cocktail-sized pork pie.
Quiches, all	RED	High in fat, saturated fat and calories. A small portion is a 100g slice.
Sausage roll	RED	High in calories, fat and saturated fat. A small portion is one mini sausage roll.
Vegetable pies and pasties	RED	High in fat and calories. A small portion is a 100g slice.

READY MEALS AND TAKEAWAYS

Ready Meals		
Any shop-bought, ready meal containing no more than 10g fat per portion (check label)	AMBER	If the ready meal contains little vegetable, add a salad. Try to limit ready meals to once or twice a week. Try to choose meals with no more than 0.5g salt per 100g

Any other shop-bought ready meal	RED	Try to avoid.
Ready salads, containing no more than 10g fat and 300 calories per portion	AMBER	Use ready salads as a quick lunch. Try to choose salads with no more than 0.5g salt per 100g. A medium portion contains up to 300 calories per pack.
Any other shop-bought ready salad	RED	Try to avoid.
Ready sandwiches, containing no more than 10g fat and 300 calories per portion.	AMBER	Use as a quick lunch. Try to choose sandwiches with no more than 0.5g salt per 100g and those containing plenty of salad. Follow with fruit.
Any other shop-bought sandwich	RED	Try to avoid.
Pizza: deep-pan, all	RED	The thick white crust makes the pizza very high in calories and can cause bloating. Best to choose a thin-crust version. A small portion is one three-inch slice.
vegetable, thin/crispy	AMBER	Can be a good source of nutrients. A medium portion is a third of a ten-inch pizza.

marinara, thin/crispy	AMBER	As vegetable pizza.
meat, all kinds	RED	Meat-topped pizzas can be high in fat and calories. Try to choose vegetable or fish varieties. A small portion is one three-inch slice.
three cheese, all kinds	RED	Pizzas with a higher than average amount of cheese topping are likely to be high in fat, saturated fat and calories. Try to choose vegetable or fish varieties. A small portion is one three-inch slice.

Takeaways

Any takeaway meal, containing more than 20g fat per portion, including pizza, Chinese, Thai, Indian, Greek, fish and chips	RED	If you don't know the fat content, it counts as RED. A small portion of a RED takeaway is 150g *or* try to eat no more than one a month. Note: Some takeaway chains will provide nutrition information for you, e.g. in a leaflet.
Any takeaway meal containing less than 20g fat and 500 calories per portion, eaten as a main meal	AMBER	Some takeaway chains will provide nutrition information for you. Limit AMBER takeaways to no more than once a week and try to choose those containing no more than 0.5g salt per 100g. Try to choose those containing vegetables and/or salad and follow with fruit.

SAUCES, DRESSINGS AND CONDIMENTS

Sauces/dips		
Cheese sauce: full-fat	RED	High in fat and calories and probably salt. A small portion is 2 level tablespoons.
low-fat	AMBER	Lower in fat and calories, but may be high in salt. A medium portion is 3 tablespoons.
Guacamole	AMBER	This avocado sauce is high in mono-unsaturated fat and nutrients. A medium portion is 1 heaped tablespoon.
Hollandaise	RED	Very high in fat and calories. A small portion is 1 level dessert-spoon.
Hummus – see Vegetable Proteins and Pulses		

Mayonnaise:
  full-fat
  reduced-fat
	RED
	AMBER
		As hollandaise.
		Lower in fat and calories. A medium portion is 1 level tablespoon.

Salad cream	AMBER	A medium portion is 1 dessert-spoon.
Vegetable salsas, commercial and home-made	GREEN	Low in fat and calories. Can make a useful side dish for a plain meal, e.g. a grill.

Vegetable sauces, home-made	GREEN	Home-made tomato sauces are low in fat and calories, and are useful for pasta and grills.
Vegetable sauces, commercial, containing no more than 60 calories per 100ml	AMBER	Ideal for pasta. A medium portion is 100ml.
Tahini – see Nuts and Seeds		
Taramasalata – see Fish and Seafood		
Tomato ketchup	AMBER	Low in fat and contains anti-cancer lycopene. May be high in salt. A medium portion is l tablespoon.

Dressings

Blue cheese dressing	RED	High in fat, saturates and salt. A small portion is 1 level dessertspoon.
Fat-free salad dressings, all	AMBER	May be high in salt so should be used carefully. A medium portion is 1 tablespoon.
French dressing, traditional with olive oil	AMBER	Commercial French dressing may be high in salt so use with caution. If making your own, salt can be reduced to a

		minimum. A medium portion is 1 tablespoon.
Full-fat dressings, all, other than French dressing	RED	Dressings such as Caesar are high in fat, calories and salt. A small portion is 1 level dessertspoon.

Condiments and preserves

BBQ sauce, brown sauce	RED	Low in fat but sometimes high in sugar and salt. A medium portion is 1 dessertspoon.
Burger relish	RED	As BBQ.
Coconut milk, skimmed	AMBER	Low in fat and a good addition to curries. A medium portion is 2 tablespoons.
Fruit relishes, e.g. cranberry, redcurrant	AMBER	Fat-free but high in sugar. A medium portion is 1 dessertspoon.
Herbs, fresh, frozen or dried	GREEN	Fresh herbs provide useful vitamins, minerals and anti-oxidants. Dried herbs contain few nutrients but are calorie-free and can add flavour to low-salt foods.
Jam	RED	Frequent use of jam encourages a sweet tooth. A small portion is 1–2 teaspoons.
Lemon/lime juice	GREEN	Adds piquancy to dishes and contains vitamin C.
Mustard, all types	AMBER	A useful flavour enhancer for many savouries.

Mango chutney	RED	Very high in sugar as are most curry-type chutneys. A small portion is 1–2 teaspoons.
Passata (sieved tomatoes)	GREEN	A very useful low-fat, high-nutrient condiment for many sauces and savoury dishes.
Peanut butter – see Nuts and Seeds		
Piccalilli	GREEN	Low in fat and calories, a useful relish.
Pickled onions	GREEN	As piccalilli.
Pickled beetroot	GREEN	As piccalilli.
Salt	RED	Avoid adding salt to cooking and at table. Try to avoid salty foods containing more than 0.5g salt per 100g.
Soya sauce	RED	Low in calories and fat free but high in salt, so go carefully. Reduced-salt soya sauce is a better option but it still contains high salt levels. A portion is 1 dessertspoon.
Spices, fresh, or dried	GREEN	Fresh spices are an excellent replacement for salt in cooking, and are a rich source of anti-oxidants and other disease-preventing chemicals. Don't keep dried ground spices too long, as they lose their potency.

Stock cubes or bouillon	AMBER	Choose low-salt varieties. Often high in additives.
Sweet pickles and chutneys	RED	Low in fat but often high in sugar and calories. A small portion is l dessertspoon.
Tomato purée	GREEN	A useful source of lycopene; good as a flavouring and thickener for many dishes.
Tomatoes, sun-blush and sun-dried	GREEN	Add flavour and texture to many savoury dishes.
Vinegar, all types	GREEN	Very low in calories and adds interest to many dishes. Balsamic vinegar is a good sweetener.
Worcestershire sauce	AMBER	Low in calories but high in salt. A medium portion is 1 dessertspoon.

SNACKS

Bombay Mix	RED	Very high in salt and calories. A small portion is one very small handful.
Crisps, potato: full-fat	RED	Weight for weight, high in calories as well as fat and salt. A small portion is one 25g bag. Try to limit to one packet a week.
lower-fat	RED	A small portion is one 25g bag. Try to limit to two packets a week. Note: all potato crisps are high on the glycaemic index.

Oriental mix	RED	These Chinese crackers are very high in salt and calories. Best avoided. A small portion is one very small handful.
Popcorn, plain or sweet	RED	Perhaps better than crisps but still offering little nutrition and high on the glycaemic index. May be high in salt. A small portion is one small bag.
Pretzels	AMBER	Lower in calories, fat and salt than some snacks. A medium portion is 30g. Best limited to two or three times a week.
Tortilla chips	RED	High in calories, fat and salt. A small portion is one small handful. Best limited to once or twice a week.

SOUPS

Home-made vegetable or pulse soups (see recipes)	GREEN	Fresh vegetable soup made with minimal fat is an excellent standby for when you are hungry.
Chilled-counter soups, containing no cream and up to 6g fat per 300ml serving	AMBER	A good standby for occasional use but try to choose vegetable or pulse varieties. A medium portion is one 300ml serving.
Chilled-counter soups,	RED	High in fat and calories. A small portion is 100ml.

creamed and/or containing more than 6g fat per 300ml serving		
Tinned soups	RED	Usually high in salt and low in vegetables. Choose fresh or chilled-counter soups for preference. A small portion is 100ml.
Packet-dried soups	RED	Usually very high in salt and additives. Best avoided.

VEGETABLES

Artichoke hearts, fresh or canned in water	GREEN	Good low-fat addition to salads and soups. Avoid those canned in brine.
Artichoke, Jerusalem	GREEN	Makes a good substitute for potatoes with fewer calories.
Asparagus, fresh or canned in water	GREEN	High in vitamin E and glycosides, which may help arthritis.
Aubergine	GREEN	Can soak up a lot of fat if you are not careful – brush with oil and bake or grill.
Avocado	AMBER	High in fat of the mono-unsaturated variety, rich in vitamin E. One medium portion equals half a medium avocado.

Bamboo shoots, canned in water	GREEN	A useful addition to oriental dishes.
Corn:		
baby or large cobs	GREEN	High in vitamin C and fibre.
kernels, fresh or frozen	GREEN	As cobs.
canned in brine	AMBER	High in salt and lower in vitamin C. A medium portion is 100g.
Beans:		
broad	GREEN	High in fibre, vitamins and minerals.
French	GREEN	High in vitamin C.
runner	GREEN	High in vitamin C.
Beans, dried – see Vegetable Proteins and Pulses		
Beansprouts	GREEN	High in vitamin C and folate. Best used raw.
Beetroot	GREEN	High in folate and potassium.
Broccoli	GREEN	High in vitamin C, folate, and carotenoids and glucosinolates, which fight cancer.
Brussels sprouts	GREEN	High in vitamin C, folate and fibre. Another cancer-fighting vegetable.
Cabbage:		
dark green	GREEN	High in vitamin C, folate,

		carotenoids and fibre. Also contains cancer-fighting plant chemicals.
white	GREEN	Contains fewer carotenoids than those with dark green leaves.
red	GREEN	Good source of folate and vitamin C. Contains the carotenoid lycopene, also found in tomatoes.
Carrots	GREEN	High in beta-carotene, which aids vision and also fights heart disease and cancer.
Cauliflower	GREEN	High in folate, vitamin C and glucosinolates.
Celery	GREEN	Contains a plant chemical that can help lower blood pressure. A natural diuretic.
Chicory	GREEN	Contains anti-cancer compounds, which gives it its slightly bitter flavour
Chinese leaves	GREEN	A good source of folate and vitamin C.
Courgettes	GREEN	High in beta-carotene, vitamin C and potassium.
Cucumber	GREEN	A diuretic.
Endive	GREEN	All types contain plant chemicals that can fight cancer.
Fennel, Florence	GREEN	High in fibre and potassium.

Garlic	GREEN	Very high in compounds that help fight disease. Giant garlic can be used as a vegetable. Most potent when lightly cooked only – or raw.
Kale	GREEN	High in vitamins C and E, carotenoids and cancer-fighting glucosinolates.
Leek	GREEN	A member of the onion family, with similar properties.
Lettuce: cos/Little Gem	GREEN	The outer leaves are high in plant nutrients, including folate. High in fibre and the plant chemical zeaxanthin, which helps protect eyesight.
iceberg	GREEN	Contains few nutrients. (The paler the leaves of vegetables, the fewer nutrients they tend to contain.)
red-leaved	GREEN	Red tinges mean higher levels of carotenoids and flavonoids for protection against disease.
Marrow	GREEN	Its very high water content means fewer nutrients per serving.
Mushrooms: fresh	GREEN	Dark-coloured, wild and speciality mushrooms contain high levels of plant chemicals that can fight cancer. A good source of protein and B vitamins. White button mushrooms contain few nutrients.

breaded	RED	When cooked, these are high in fat and calories. A small portion is five breaded mushrooms.
mushroom pâté	AMBER	A good pâté for vegetarians but it can be high in fat. A medium portion is 50g.
Okra	GREEN	Very high in soluble fibre, which can lower levels of LDL cholesterol.
Onions: fresh	GREEN	High in vitamin C, potassium and compounds that can help beat high blood pressure and high cholesterol levels. They contain sulphurs that may fight cancer, and several other beneficial compounds.
breaded or battered	RED	High in calories and fat when fried. A small portion is two onion rings.
Parsnips	GREEN	High in carbohydrate but not particularly high in calories; high in fibre, vitamin C, folate and iron.
Peas: fresh or frozen	GREEN	High in fibre, carotenoids, potassium and vitamin C.
canned in water	GREEN	Canned peas contain less vitamin C than fresh.
mangetout	GREEN	As fresh peas.
mushy, canned	GREEN	Contain no vitamin C but are quite high in iron. Salt levels moderate.

sugar snap	GREEN	As fresh peas.
Peppers, fresh	GREEN	All peppers are high in vitamin C and carotenoids, as well as containing a natural painkiller, capsaicin. Red peppers contain the highest levels of nutrients.

Potatoes:
  boiled or
  baked
	AMBER	High in starch but not too high in calories. A good source of potassium, vitamin C and fibre. A medium portion is 150g. Boiled potatoes are lower on the glycaemic index than mashed or baked.

chipped, all kinds	RED	High in fat and calories. Oven-baked chips contain less fat than deep-fried. A small portion is 100g.

mashed:
  with butter
  and milk
	RED	Can be high in fat and calories. A small portion is 100g.

with skimmed milk	AMBER	Higher on the glycaemic index than boiled potatoes. A medium portion is 150g.
potato salad	RED	High in fat and calories. A small portion is 50g.
Pumpkin	GREEN	See Marrow.
Radish	GREEN	High in potassium.
Rocket	GREEN	High in vitamin C, carotenoids and plant chemicals.
Sea vegetables	GREEN	High in calcium and fibre and a source of B12 for vegans. Can be

		high in salt so wash thoroughly and don't add salt in cooking.
Spinach, fresh or frozen	GREEN	High in carotenoids, vitamins C and E, folate and fibre. The oxalic acid it contains hinders mineral absorption. Contains compounds that protect vision and eyes.
Spring greens	GREEN	As Cabbage, dark green.
Squash	GREEN	Orange-fleshed varieties are high in carotenoids with a good flavour. A good source of vitamins C, E and potassium.
Swede	GREEN	A good source of fibre, vitamin C and carotenoids. Contains cancer-fighting chemicals, as do cabbage and other brassicas.
Sweet potatoes	AMBER	High in carbohydrate, rich in vitamins C and E, fibre, carotenoids and potassium. A medium portion is 150g.
Tomatoes: canned	GREEN	A useful standby and rich in lycopene.
fresh	GREEN	A good source of vitamins C and E, carotenoids and potassium.
Tomato purée, passata, sunblush, sundried tomatoes		See Sauces, Dressings and Condiments.

Turnips	GREEN	A good source of fibre, vitamin C and glucosinolates.
Vegetable crispbakes	RED	When cooked, high in fat and calories. A small portion is one small crispbake or half a large one.
Watercress	GREEN	Rich in vitamin C, E, iron and plant chemicals that fight cancer.
Yams	AMBER	High in starch, these white-fleshed root vegetables are fairly high in calories but also contain good amounts of fibre and potassium. They are lower on the glycaemic index than potatoes and can be used for baking or mashing. A medium portion is 150g.

VEGETABLE PROTEINS AND PULSES

Baked beans in tomato sauce:		
standard	AMBER	Can be high in sugar and salt but also contains lycopene, fibre and various other nutrients. A medium portion is 200g.
low-salt, low-sugar	AMBER	A good choice when cutting salt and sugar levels.
Bean burgers	AMBER	A good high-fibre protein food but may be relatively high in fat. A medium portion is one quarter pounder.

Butter-beans, dried or canned in water	GREEN	High in fibre, soluble fibre and potassium. Avoid all pulses canned in brine.
Cannellini beans	GREEN	As butter-beans.
Chickpeas: dried or canned in water	GREEN	A good source of vitamin E and fibre.
hummus	AMBER	Commercial brands can be high in fat and calories. See the recipe on page 121 for a lower-fat version. A medium portion is 1 heaped tablespoon.
felafel (chickpea patties)	AMBER	Can be high in fat and salt and calories but a useful item for vegans. A medium portion is two patties.
Haricot beans	GREEN	As butter-beans.
Lentils, dried or canned in water	GREEN	High in fibre. Green and brown varieties contain more nutrients than red ones. All are a good source of iron and potassium.
lentil dhal	AMBER	Can be high in fat. A medium portion is 2 tablespoons.
lentil pâté	AMBER	Can be high in fat but useful for vegans. A medium portion is 50g.
Pulses, dried, all kinds	GREEN	Healthy sources of protein, which may lower levels of LDL cholesterol. Cook according

		to packet instructions; otherwise, they can be toxic.
Quorn: pieces, mince, chunks	GREEN	High in protein, fibre and zinc. Very low in fat and calories. Good for casseroles, as takes up flavours well.
sausages, uncoated fillet	GREEN	As pieces.
other, e.g. Quorn ready meals	AMBER or RED	See Ready Meals for guidelines.
Red kidney beans, dried or canned in water	GREEN	Very high in fibre, soluble fibre, folate, potassium and iron.
Refried beans	AMBER	High in fat and calories. A medium portion is 1 tablespoon.
Soya beans, dried or canned in water	GREEN	Contain complete protein on a par with meat protein; may help prevent breast cancer and heart disease. Very high in fibre, soluble fibre, folate, vitamin E and a range of minerals including iron and magnesium.
soya mince	GREEN	As soya beans.
Soya milk and yoghurt, plain	GREEN	Dairy-free alternative to cow's milk and yoghurt. Choose calcium-fortified brands.
Split peas, dried	GREEN	Contain fewer nutrients than other pulses.

Tofu, silken or firm	GREEN	A low-fat vegan protein food, and a good source of calcium. Takes up other flavours well. Contains only a little fibre and nutrients.
TVP mince	AMBER	This minced-meat substitute can be high in fat. A medium portion is 100g reconstituted weight.

7 GET MOVING

'Oh no! Not the exercise bit,' I hear you saying. By now almost everybody probably knows that it is 'diet *and* exercise' that are the keys to losing weight and keeping it off.

But for many people the 'exercise bit' is harder to do and to maintain than the dieting.

I know, from talking to people and from independent studies that have been done, that two of the main reasons for this are:

1. lack of time
2. lack of incentive because exercise is perceived as boring and/or too difficult

In this short chapter I hope to provide you with the motivation and the wherewithal to take up some regular activity because, as you will find out here, it will make it much easier to shed that weight and not put it back on. Not only that but it is going to make you feel better and help you to better health and, possibly, a longer life.

Weight Loss and Activity – the Facts

'There is little doubt that the nation as a whole is not as active as it should be. Levels of activity in the UK are below the

European average, which is part of the explanation for higher obesity rates.'

In his April 2004 report on exercise and health, *At Least Five a Week,* the UK's Chief Medical Officer, Sir Liam Donaldson, agreed with this statement from the Commons Select Committee, writing that low levels of physical activity are a significant factor in the dramatic increase in the prevalence of obesity. Indeed, the links between activity and weight control have been verified time and time again.

As we saw in Chapter 1, to lose weight you need to create an energy deficit – providing your body with fewer calories (energy) than it needs to maintain its current weight. One way you can do this is by eating fewer calories. The other is by increasing your energy expenditure. Energy expenditure equals activity, exercise, movement, using your body – call it what you like but the fact is that, for most people, *more* energy expenditure is a vital part of getting the weight off and keeping it off.

Among a wealth of research, a recent study published in the *International Journal of Obesity,* for example, has shown that people with higher levels of energy expenditure tend to have a lower fat mass. Another, published in the *Journal of the American Medical Association,* found that overweight women who did the most exercise lost twice as much weight as those who did less.

Here are the ways in which activity helps to control weight and shape:

It burns calories

Several studies have shown that increasing exercise levels alone can result in moderate, steady weight loss. If you don't diet but simply increase your activity levels on a regular basis, you may lose between one and two pounds a month, depending on the amount and type of exercise that you do.

A simple rule of thumb is that for every 3,500 calories extra that you burn up (over and above your previous exercise levels), you will lose approximately one pound of body fat. So, to lose one pound of body fat a month, for example, you would need to exercise to burn off an extra 115 calories a day – a level that can be achieved by moderately brisk walking for 30 minutes.

It helps conserve lean tissue

When you lose weight, by whatever means, you lose both body fat and lean tissue – more commonly called muscle. Research shows that if you lose weight by dieting alone without increased activity, you will tend to lose a higher proportion of lean tissue. However, losing weight through exercise alone, or through a combination of diet and exercise, results in conservation of more muscle with proportionately more fat lost.

This is important in the long term, because lean tissue needs more energy than fat tissue – in other words, it burns more calories. The greater the amount of lean tissue in your body the higher your metabolic rate will be. This in turn means that in the long term you will have less trouble maintaining a healthy weight, because you will continue to burn more calories (as long as your levels of lean tissue are maintained).

It is thought that this fat/lean ratio is one of the main reasons why long-term 'yo-yo' dieters have trouble keeping weight off. Every time that you diet without also increasing the amount of exercise that you take, you lose a little more lean tissue. When the weight comes back on again, your fat/lean ratio increases. Each time that you go back on another diet – *without* also raising your exercise levels, this fat/lean ratio increases a little more, reducing your metabolic rate further with every new diet.

Lean tissue can be conserved by various types of exercise – of which more later.

It raises the metabolic rate by other means

Studies show that when you exercise – for example aerobic exercise such as walking or cycling, or even resistance exercise such as working with weights – your metabolic rate is raised for some time *after* you finish exercising. This means that if you exercise regularly, you will burn more calories even when resting. The effect is not simply due to any long-term increase in lean tissue.

It can improve your shape

Regular exercise can improve the way you look – making you more firm and toned-looking – and it can also reduce your waist size. This waist reduction can have health benefits (see below) while a better body shape can make you appear slimmer than you actually are.

Different types of exercise can have different effects on your body's appearance. For example, walking and cycling can tone the leg muscles, whilst working with dumb-bells can tone your upper body.

Heart–lung fitness increases your fat-burning capacity

Once your cardiovascular fitness has improved via aerobic exercise, research shows that your body will be able to burn more body fat per exercise session than if you were unfit. In other words, being fitter means that it is easier to stay slim!

Exercise boosts self-esteem

Once you begin to take regular exercise you get on a 'positive' circuit. When you exercise you feel good about yourself – you are 'being good'. This in turn helps you to control your eating. You set up a circle of motivation and boosted self-esteem, which together strengthen your resolve to lose weight.

Exercise helps you stay slim for life

There is plenty of research to show that people who lose weight and who manage to keep it off over long periods of time also exercise regularly. Few people who don't exercise manage to stay slim over time.

Health and Activity – the Facts

The Chief Medical Officer has described physical inactivity as a 'serious and increasing public health problem'.

It is estimated that our sedentary lifestyles cost the NHS approximately £8.2 billion a year because of all the diseases and health problems that occur as a direct consequence, or as a partial consequence, of inactivity. The Wanless report, *Securing Good Health for the Whole Population*, written for the government and published in February 2004, stated: 'Adults who are physically active are 20–30 per cent less likely to die prematurely.'

As we have seen inactivity contributes to overweight and obesity which, in turn, as we have seen on page 21, is associated with a wide variety of medical problems. But even if you are not overweight, being unfit and sedentary is linked with around 20 health problems and diseases. No wonder that physical inactivity has been described by the World Health Organisation as one of the ten leading causes of death in developed countries.

Activity can help you to health in all the following ways:

Decreased risk of cardiovascular disease

The link between lack of exercise and heart disease and stroke is as strong as the link between those conditions and smoking. Studies have indicated that over one-third of all cases of heart disease in the UK are directly attributable to lack of activity. They also indicate that fit people are 50 per cent less at risk of dying from heart disease or stroke than those who are unfit. One US study found that women who walked daily for half an hour had 30 per cent less risk of stroke.

Cardiovascular (aerobic-type) exercise, such as brisk walking or cycling, helps to keep the heart, respiratory system and circulation healthy by:

→ **slowing down the rate at which the heart beats**
→ **reducing blood pressure**
→ **improving the lipid (fat) profile of the blood**
→ **decreasing insulin sensitivity (see diabetes, below)**

Decreased risk of diabetes

Type 2 diabetes (once called 'mid-life onset diabetes') is increasing among UK adults and is now even seen in young teenagers. Regularly active people reduce their risk of developing diabetes by up to 50 per cent, whilst diabetics can help control their condition via exercise. Similarly, for people with insulin resistance, often described as the precursor to Type 2 diabetes, exercise also has a beneficial effect.

Decreased risk of osteoporosis

To help prevent the onset of osteoporosis – reduction in the density of bone mineral, which often occurs in old age but can happen at any time – regular weight-bearing exercise is recommended. Activities such as lifting weights, walking and jogging are all weight-bearing. Exercise helps to increase bone density in the young, can help conserve it in adults and can slow down the mineral loss in old age.

Decreased risk of skeletal problems such as osteoarthritis and low back pain

Regular low- or moderate-intensity exercise and flexibility work can help to prevent or minimise the pain and stiffness of arthritis, and can also help strengthen the spine and the body core. People with weak stomach muscles and an inflexible spine are more likely to suffer from back problems.

Decreased risk of cancer

Regular exercise is linked with a reduction in the risk of getting all cancers. There appears to be a particularly strong protective effect for breast cancer after the menopause, and colon cancer. Indeed, the World Health Organisation estimates that inactivity is responsible for 16–17 per cent of all colon cancers and 11 per cent of all breast cancers.

Decreased risk of mental problems

As well as all the physical benefits of exercise, we now know that three of the big mental 'curses' of modern living – stress, anxiety and depression – can all be treated, or at least improved, via an exercise programme. Other lifestyle problems such as insomnia and anger can also be decreased or minimised with activity. Sometimes it is these, unthought-of benefits that actually motivate people to continue with exercise.

Once we begin to realise how much better we feel, physically and mentally, when we exercise, it is hard to stop!

So Why Don't We Exercise?

When you look at all the benefits of exercise both for weight control and our present and future health, it is almost incomprehensible that most of us just don't do it.

And yet the research paints a picture of a very idle nation, that is also becoming more inactive as the years go by.

Look at the figures:

WALKING

The average UK person walks around 189 miles a year (an annual reduction of sixty-six miles in the past twenty-five years) and a current total equivalent to around half a mile – or a quarter of an hour – a day.

CYCLING

Fifty years ago, people in the UK annually cycled a total of approximately 23 billion kilometres (15.3 million miles). Now we cycle only 4 billion kilometres (2.6 billion miles).

As walking and cycling have traditionally been our main forms of exercise, it is no wonder that now only around a third of adults do enough exercise for basic health. Less than half of us partake in any sport more than a dozen times a year. By the time the current generation leave school, 70 per cent of them have given up all sport, so the future picture looks even more bleak for our physical health. There is more about children and exercise on pages 255–7.

Many of the reasons for this decline in physical activity are obvious:

→ **The growth of motorised transport offers fewer opportunities and less incentive to walk or cycle.**

→ **Our mechanised and 'labour-saving' lifestyles create less need to burn calories by climbing stairs, cleaning the house, doing the DIY or gardening.**

→ **To make matters worse, only 10 per cent of women and 20 per cent of men now have active jobs.**

→ **We all watch twice the amount of TV that we did forty years ago.**

→ **More and more leisure-time activities – such as web surfing, computer games and eating out – are sedentary rather than active.**

→ **Finally, our busy lifestyles persuade us that there is less time to exercise. And, as we get out of the habit of exercising, we find it more and more difficult to motivate ourselves to return to it.**

We need very compelling reasons to alter our lifestyles to become more active. Physical health, easier weight maintenance, longer life, better sense of well-being – I think these are strong enough reasons. Don't you?

How Much Activity Do We Really Need?

'Current Department of Health advice is for individuals to take 30 minutes of moderate intensity exercise at least five days a week. Only around 37 per cent of men and 25 per cent of women currently achieve this target.'

What is most interesting is that it doesn't take a huge amount of exercise – or a huge amount of effort, 'going for the burn', getting exhausted, etc. – to achieve real improvements in your health via exercise. Let's face it, a half-hour spent being active five times a week is not a great deal of effort in exchange for the benefits to be gained.

(Activity levels recommended for children are slightly different: see page 255.)

The Chief Medical Officer in his report on physical activity (*At Least Five a Week*) says that a little more than five periods of 30 minutes may be needed to prevent obesity in some people, in which case he suggests increasing the time spent exercising to 45 minutes.

In other words, 30 minutes five times a week is all that is needed to help most people to improved health, whether or not they are overweight. Some people (depending on factors such as how much they eat) may need to do more if they want to use exercise as a weight-control tool. For them, 45 minutes a day may be a better goal to aim for.

> ### Remember:
> • A half-hour walk can burn around 115 extra calories so, at five to seven times a week, this would mean a monthly weight loss of about one pound for many people.

Easy Ways to Meet Your Target

There are two ways in which you can increase your activity levels.

The first is to take up **organised exercise**, or increase the amount you do. For example:

→ going for a leisure-time walk or cycle ride (perhaps in shorter bursts, such as two 15-minute sessions)
→ going to the gym
→ taking up an organised sport such as football, or a solo sport such as swimming

The second is to **become more active** in your everyday life. For example:

→ using the stairs instead of taking the lift
→ using the car a little less for short journeys and walking or cycling instead

This book, as you may have noticed by now, is mainly concerned with weight loss and weight maintenance. As we have already seen, 30 minutes a day (or more for some people) may be needed to achieve that goal through exercise (combined with diet).

Therefore my strategy for you is as follows:

→ **Thirty minutes daily (or for at least five days a week) of some organised activity. This does not necessarily have to be done all at once but can be done in shorter modules, as long as they add up to a 30-minute total. By organised, I mean an activity for which you create a 'slot' (or slots) in your life and recognise that it is your 'exercise time'.**
→ ***Plus* making a real effort to increase your activity levels in everyday life. This could easily add another 15–30 minutes of activity to your daily total.**

These measures could mean that you burn an extra 150 calories a day or more. Combined with your diet, this will make a very real difference to your weight loss and, afterwards, to your weight maintenance.

Of course, the big question is: how do you achieve those

goals? How do you motivate yourself to begin? How do you stick at it?

In order to achieve your goals, we need to make sure that the structured activity you do is something you like doing (or at least, don't mind doing) and that it is practical in terms of fitting it into your life.

And we need to make sure that the increased activity in your everyday life, part two of our strategy, is achieved in ways that don't impinge too much on your lifestyle.

For both categories, I hope that the next few pages will provide the answers. But we also need to ensure that there is a simple way to encourage you to do it. And there is – a very simple way, which we will discuss shortly, under 'Making it better'.

First, let's look at your structured 30 minutes of daily activity.

Walking

Most of the research on activity that has been published in recent years comes to the same conclusion: that the best form of exercise for health, weight control and what the experts quaintly term 'compliance' (meaning that you will actually do it!) is good old walking. And, indeed, it has a lot going for it, which is why it is my activity of choice for most of you.

The practical benefits of walking

→ It can be done by almost everyone and few if any new skills need to be learnt at the start. Most of us have had quite a lot of practice over the years.

→ It can be done almost anywhere, at almost any time, and it requires little planning.

→ Unless you want to, you don't need to travel before you can do it.

→ You can do it at times when you only have a few minutes to spare.

→ It is very low cost.

→ It requires very little in the way of special equipment.

→ It can be done alone or with others.

→ It can be done all year round with few exceptions.

→ It is generally very safe.

→ Doing it is unlikely to cause you embarrassment or to draw attention to yourself.

→ It can be done by all the family.

→ It can be competitive or non-competitive.

The health benefits of walking

→ It can be easily tailored to fit your own level of fitness and it can even be done by people who are very unfit or obese.

→ It is easy to improve your fitness by increasing your walking speed or by other means such as walking uphill instead of on the flat.

→ It is unlikely to cause joint or back problems or other injuries because it is low impact.

→ It can help strengthen the leg and stomach muscles, which can improve body shape, and it can increase lean tissue, which may increase your metabolic rate.

→ It is one of the most suitable forms of exercise for people with high blood pressure, and can even reduce it.

→ It is one of the most suitable forms of exercise for people with cardiovascular disease or circulatory problems.

→ It helps to improve the blood lipid profile, reducing 'bad' LDL cholesterol for instance and helping to increase levels of 'good' HDL cholesterol.

→ It can increase insulin sensitivity and is perhaps the best form of exercise for people with insulin resistance or diabetes.

→ It is good for the mind. Walking can lift depression, relax you, calm you down, disperse tension and aggression, and enhance your mood.

Walking plans

The great advantage of walking to achieve your daily exercise target is that you can virtually write your own timetable. Here I suggest two ways in which you can achieve the total but as long as you do the right amount of walking over seven (or at least five) days of the week or more,* you can do it to suit yourself. You can even do three 10-minute bursts on some days, if you prefer.

* Very unfit people should build up to this level gradually — see Health and Safety tips below.

PLAN ONE – BEGINNERS

Tuesday: Morning, 15 minutes; evening, 15 minutes.
Wednesday: Morning, 15 minutes; evening, 15 minutes.
Thursday: Morning, 15 minutes; evening, 15 minutes.
Saturday: Morning, 30 minutes.
Sunday: Afternoon, 30 minutes.

PLAN TWO

This is very simple: 30 minutes every evening of the week *or* 15 minutes every morning and every evening of the week.

How simple do those plans look? All you need to do now is

address a few moments to considering your walking style and you are ready to go.

Tips to achieve maximum benefits

→ Walk with your arms swinging moderately at your sides, in an upright stance with stomach and bottom tucked in. Aim for a loose, long stride.

→ Walk at a pace that gets you feeling slightly puffed out for benefit to your cardiovascular system. You should still be able to talk while you walk, but you should be conscious of your heart and lungs working somewhat. As the weeks progress, you will need to walk faster (by speeding up your pace and/or by taking longer strides) to achieve this feeling. And finally, as you get a lot fitter, you will be able to exert yourself even more, for instance by walking uphill.

Note: If you dawdle along, you won't achieve the health benefits. On the other hand, you shouldn't walk so fast that you have to stop to regain your breath.

Wherever you walk and whatever stage of your walking programme you are at, and however fit or unfit you are – you must remember that you need to keep your body in a state of being 'slightly puffed out' while you walk. That way you will always know that you are improving your fitness level and burning optimum calories.

Once you reach the stage where you are walking at your fastest, up steep hills, and you aren't in that 'slightly puffed out' state, you will know that ordinary walking has done all it can for your fitness. If you want to increase your fitness further, you will need to switch to a more demanding sport such as running. However, if you continue to walk, you will still burn calories, of course, and you will maintain your current fitness level – but you won't *increase* your fitness. But by that stage, the main benefits of your walking programme for your health will have been achieved – and for most of us there is no real need to increase fitness levels further.

Health and Safety tips

→ If you are extremely unfit, begin by walking for 20 minutes three times a week, then build up to 30 minutes four times a week. Finally do 30 minutes for at least five days a week as per Plan One above.

→ Wear comfortable, suitable footwear such as trainers especially designed for walking. A thick, padded or air-layered sole is important to prevent jarring and joint damage, particularly if you do a lot of walking on hard surfaces such as concrete.

→ Wear comfortable clothes such as tracksuit bottoms and a T-shirt with a sweatshirt over – layers are best as you will warm up during your walk and may want to remove a layer. A sweatshirt can be tied around your waist.

→ Take a bottle of water to swig from during the walk (especially important for longer walks and in warm weather). You can buy bottle holders which clip around your waist.

→ Avoid walking after dark, particularly if you are alone.

→ Don't push yourself so hard that you get really out of breath and need to stop – this is working too hard. You should be able to continue walking without stopping.

→ Don't walk so hard that you feel any pain, e.g. in your chest, lungs or joints.

→ Warm up at the start of the walk by walking moderately for 2–3 minutes. Cool down at the end of the walk similarly.

→ Leg-stretching exercises at the end of a walk can help to prevent muscular stiffness. (The four classic stretches appear on pages 264–5.)

→ Don't walk if you are ill.

Exercise in Everyday Life

Now we look at ways to increase activity in your daily life, to achieve a further 15–30 minutes of exercise over and above what you currently do.

As we have seen, modern life has made us lazy. Research shows that if we are more than a few minutes' walk away from our destination, we take the car. We do a big shop at the supermarket, so we no longer carry our food home on foot or on a bicycle.

We drive to the station to catch a train to work. We use escalators and lifts instead of stairs. Many of us live in apartments or bungalows so we get no regular exercise climbing stairs at home.

We use every labour-saving device inside the home that we can find, with the result that we are less active, use fewer calories and become gradually more unfit.

A few decades ago, we used to use manual sweepers to clean the carpets, and did heavy washing by hand, but no longer. Our main home hobby, DIY, has been made less active with the use of power tools. And our other big hobby, gardening, is also more of a doddle now as we use self-propelled mowers, power strimmers, saws and cutters.

Our leisure hours are spent watching TV, or glued to the computer, or in pubs, clubs and restaurants, rather than joining in sport or other activities. And our time at work is also spent in a more sedentary way. Few of us do manual work and the small amount of exercise that we used to get in the office, walking between desks or offices, has reduced as we stay put and send e-mails or use the phone instead.

If we work in large office blocks and complexes that have their own canteens or restaurants, we don't even need to walk outside for a lunch break.

Even on holiday many of us prefer to laze on the beach or

by the pool instead of playing beach games, swimming or sightseeing.

So what is to be done?

The best way to reverse this trend is to start by thinking of one or two ways you can put back a little of what you have lost by making resolutions.

These could be, for example:

→ I will never use a lift or escalator but always take the stairs instead.

→ I will turn off a TV programme that I find boring in good weather and either do something in the garden or walk round the park instead.

Just those two things alone could easily give you your extra 15–30 minutes' exercise a day. Then as you become fitter and/or more used to building extra activity into your life you could include one or two more resolutions – making sure they are things you really feel you can do and won't resent.

For example, if you live alone and need only small amounts of food shopping, you could make the resolution:

→ I will walk to the shop to buy my food and carry the bags home.

Or if that isn't practical, but you normally get a bus to work you could make the resolution:

→ I will leave home a few minutes earlier and walk to the bus stop one further away from my home.

Or alternatively:

➜ **I will drive to the supermarket but park my car as far away from the entrance as I can.**

Think of what you could do now. Check through all the examples above of how we have become more sedentary over the years and use them to make your own resolutions.

It will help you if you keep a written diary of your efforts to increase the amount of time you spend in activity, at least for the first couple of weeks. After that, your slightly changed routine should become just that – routine ... a habit you don't need to think about too much.

The time factor

Some of these ideas will, inevitably, take up a little more of your time than before. This will probably be true of walking rather than taking the car to the train, and also walking from the shops with your shopping.

But that needn't always be the case. I know people who live in cities who have started walking to work and it actually usually takes no longer than going by bus, tube or car, because of the levels of traffic and transport delays. For other people, some of the time spent walking is saved on time not spent looking for parking spaces, feeding meters, and so on.

On a deeper level, most people find that if they begin regular activity such as walking or some other aerobic choice, they actually find themselves more efficient with more brain power, so they save time during the working day that way. Indeed, research shows that exercise *is* good for the brain – for concentration, clear-headedness, energy and motivation.

Lastly, on the subject of making time to increase your activity, I need to point out something that to me is obvious. It is all a matter of priorities. Which is more important – your health, your shape, your weight, your future life ... or that TV programme, that complicated recipe, that clothes shopping trip?

If you are saying you really can't make the time to do 30 minutes' exercise a day, plus building a little more activity into your ordinary life, perhaps you need to take a few minutes to consider your priorities. If necessary, make a diary of how you spend a few typical days and then go through it and see what you might be able to change.

Yes, of course there are things you need to do that are more important than exercise on every day of the week – spend time with your children, for example, care for a parent, stay in touch with friends, earn a living. But there will also be things that are less important than exercise, which you could spend less time on or even relinquish. If you do that list, as suggested above, you may find out what they are. I did the same thing myself and found that I could get up half an hour or so earlier in the mornings, as I had previously simply been lying there half-awake for that time, so I wasn't getting any benefit. I also found that I was happy to take a quick shower instead of a lingering bath a few times a week.

There is almost always a way in which you can find a bit of extra time to look after your body. It is all about balance.

And as for choosing between friends and family versus exercise, I give you another thought. You could do both. Take the kids cycling or walking or playing in the park. Go power walking with your best friend or partner. Push the baby in his/her pram or buggy to help him/her sleep in the evening. Borrow a friend's dog and take it and the kids for a walk every day.

There is usually an answer if you use a bit of lateral thinking.

There are other ways you can increase your activity levels too.

Use waiting time to move

We all have times in our daily lives when we are just standing or sitting, with nothing to do, often when we are on our own. This could be waiting for a kettle or pan to boil, waiting for someone to arrive or ring, or even waiting for a train. Here are some ways you could use that 'empty' time to add a few more minutes to the amount of exercise you do each day:

→ **Do some stretching exercises while you wait for the kettle to boil.**
→ **March on the spot while you wait for someone to call back.**
→ **Walk up and down the platform if it isn't too crowded while you wait for the train to arrive.**

Use sedentary time to move

While you are watching TV you could perhaps ride an exercise bike or use a portable treadmill. As most of us watch up to four hours' TV a day, this could represent a very easy way to boost your activity level.

Recently someone invented an exercise bike that powered the TV: if you didn't pedal, you didn't watch. That was a great idea but it didn't catch on – I wonder why?

Lastly ...

Consider restarting active hobbies that you used to enjoy when younger. Things like horse-riding, table tennis, badminton – all are enjoyable and sociable activities that somehow we just get out of the habit of doing.

How to make time? Again, less TV perhaps. We are watching more and more – on average four to five hours a day – so just consider the benefits of making a swap for just 30 minutes. If you are an average viewer that represents little more than ten per cent of your total viewing time, and I believe you will gain more than you lose. You might also consider video-taping some of your favourite programmes to watch nearer bedtime, when you wouldn't want to exercise anyway.

REMEMBER!

Thirty minutes' moderate exercise a day in addition to your previous levels of exercise can help you lose about a pound in weight a month. That's nearly a stone over a year – not counting any weight loss through dieting.

Making it Better

My promise to you earlier in this chapter was that there _is_ a way to make increasing your activity levels more fun and more interesting. There is a way to get yourself motivated. A way that has worked for a lot of people both in the UK and in the USA to date.

That way is to spend around £10 by giving yourself a small present.

What is this present?

A pedometer.

'Pedometers can be a very useful tool for encouraging people to live more actively.'

A pedometer is a small electronic gadget, available from any sports shop, department store or on the internet, which measures the number of steps that you take. It can be worn on your waistband or belt and is so unobtrusive that it can be worn all day.

And what is so great about using a pedometer? From studies made to date, it seems that they can make a big difference to our willingness to get moving. The reasons for this are as follows:

→ **Research shows that they almost immediately make you more aware of the amount of exercise you take (or are not taking). Activity levels increase because motivation is increased through actually being able to see the amount of steps taken in the course of a day.**

→ It is easy to measure how well one is doing in comparison with guidelines on how many steps a day you should aim for (see below). If halfway through the day you look at your pedometer and find that you aren't doing as well as you might, it is a good incentive to increase your activity level to compensate.

→ It is easy to inject an element of competition – say, between friends or family members – to see who manages the recommended number of steps a day. This element could even be extended to give a daily or weekly reward to the person taking the most steps.

→ The system is simple to understand and operate.

→ New goals and targets can be easily set and achievements easily monitored.

How will a pedometer fit in with my activity programme?

A basic pedometer, which simply measures the number of steps you take, will cost you around £9–£10. (You can buy slightly more sophisticated models, which will also tell you the distance covered, calories burnt and how long you have been exercising, but the basic model is good enough unless you want to spend more.)

If you decide to buy a pedometer, you can set 'step' goals

for yourself, rather than simply 'time' goals (30 minutes a day of organised activity and 15–30 minutes a day of 'every-day' activity).

When you get it, all you do is spend three days wearing the pedometer from the moment you get up to the moment you go to bed, and record the number of steps you take each day, then work out your current daily average. Most fairly sedentary people find they will take from around 2,000 steps up to around 4,000 steps a day – although this can vary tremendously and some people record less than 1,000 steps.

All you do is aim to increase the number of daily steps you take – which I will call:

PLAN THREE

→ **3,000 steps is roughly equivalent to a 30-minute walking session.**

→ **1,500 steps is roughly equivalent to the extra daily 15 minutes of activity we are aiming to manage as a minimum on top of your 30 minutes of 'organised' walking.**

So your ideal increase in steps would be 4,500. (By the way, 2,000 steps are roughly equivalent to a mile walked.)

Let me give you an example.

Let's say that you record 3,500 steps in your 'test' days. This is your current base level. Your target is to increase your steps by 4,500 and thus record a total of 8,000 daily steps on average for the next week – or at least on five days a week minimum.

The extra 4,500 steps is made up as follows:

➜ **An additional 3,000 steps to equal approx. 30 minutes organised exercise.**

➜ **An additional 1,500 steps to equal approx. 15 minutes 'every-day activity' increase.**

If you choose to do an activity that isn't walking for your 30 minutes of 'organised' sessions (see below), you will instead need to record a total of just your current daily average, plus just the 1,500 extra steps.

> **Note:** Very unfit people should increase their daily steps by 500 a day for the first week, then another 500 the second week, and so on.

But if you find yourself doing *more* than your daily targets, don't be surprised! Many people end up vying with friends, colleagues at work and partners or all the family members to see who can record the most steps. Sometimes there may be a prize on offer ... The more steps you can take a day, the more calories you will burn.

> **Note:** Some 'Steps a Day' programmes advise you to take at least 10,000 steps a day – equivalent to about five miles of walking. In my experience, that is too daunting a task for many people and my 'base level steps plus 4,500' scheme is more suitable for most of us – certainly in the early weeks.

The whole point of my activity programme is to try to make increased exercise something you can cope with without feeling that it is taking over your life.

Using a pedometer doesn't suit everybody, but it does give you more freedom to exercise as and when you want.

What your step totals mean

Check this list to see how you are doing on your daily step count:

Steps taken a day	Health rating
Under 1000	Very poor
Under 2000	Poor
2–3000	Poor to average
3–4000	Average
5–7000	Good
7–10,000	Very good
Over 10,000	Excellent

Other ways to get more (enjoyable) walking into your life

→ **Dog walking.**
→ **Join an orienteering club.**
→ **Join a rambling club.**
→ **Book a walking holiday rather than a beach holiday.**

Other Types of Exercise

I will admit that walking doesn't appeal to everybody. Of course if you prefer, you can choose other forms of activity to make up your '30 minutes a day' of structured exercise.

The Commons Select Committee report on *Obesity* recommends cycling as the other ideal form of exercise.

Cycling

Cycling confers similar health benefits to those for walking and, if you cycle at a reasonable pace, you will burn approximately the same number of calories (or slightly more) than walking briskly for the same length of time.

To make your cycling more fun, and to give added incentive to get on that bike regularly (did you know that there are 20 million unused bikes in the UK?) you could attach a meter to measure your distance travelled, and aim over the weeks to increase the distance you cover in the same time.

Because cycling is a reliable means of transport, it can actualy save you a lot of time. You will soon find that it is often more convenient and quicker to use the bike than to take a car or public transport, especially if you live in a city.

Therefore you might begin cycling to work, for instance – and combine your daily exercise with a real purpose. This means that if your cycling trip to and from work takes you 30 minutes a day, you will have achieved your daily organised exercise, so you need only do your 15–30 minutes of 'increased everyday activity' in addition to this.

On the other hand, if your cycling trip to and from work takes you 45–60 minutes altogether a day, you will have already done all your exercise for the day ('organised' plus 'everyday') and need do nothing more.

When you cycle, you should aim to cycle at a pace that makes you slightly puffed out but so that you don't have to stop. You should of course also obey all the rules of the road and pay special attention to safety, wearing a helmet and light-reflective clothes. You should also make sure your bike is roadworthy, especially if it is second-hand or hasn't been used for some time. Check the brakes before you get on a road.

TIP

If you want to, of course you can combine cycling with walking to make up your daily exercise.

And some more ...

Various other activities are suitable for your 30-minutes a day organised exercise. These include:

SWIMMING

You either love it or you don't. If you live near a pool and used to enjoy swimming, give it a try. If possible, pick a time of day when the pool isn't busy, otherwise you will find it hard to swim continuously for long enough to count as your 30 minutes. If you are unfit, believe me, it will be impossible to swim for 30 minutes anyway – you will have to build up your times sensibly over a period of weeks.

(Once you are in the water, by the way, use the rest of your 30 minutes to do some stretching exercises at the edge of the pool.)

DANCING

This is something almost everyone enjoys and it can be as strenuous as you want it to be. Obviously, the faster dances burn more calories than the slow ones – so aim for 30 minutes of energetic dancing to count as your session.

AEROBICS CLASSES

If you can't get near a dance hall, aerobics classes are

similar in that they are done to music and are – usually – enjoyable. Pick a class to suit your current fitness level.

ROLLERBLADING

This doesn't burn quite as many calories as brisk walking, but comes close and can be great fun.

THE GYM

Recent research reveals that, each year, half a million Britons join a gym – and give up going within a month. So if you want to try getting fit on the treadmill or the exercise bike, it may be better to 'pay as you go' rather than shelling out for a whole year's membership.

If you have room at home you could perhaps buy a **treadmill** or an **exercise bik**e – but again, many millions of these pieces of equipment lie unused in the cupboard under the stairs.

If you use them, however, they will get you fit and help you burn the calories just as well as ordinary walking or cycling. My advice, as someone who knows from personal experience, is that you should buy the best you can afford, with all the motivation tools such as built-in programmes, extensive electronic displays, a good incline for treadmills and plenty of variables for resistance for bikes. These really do help you stick to it. And you should record your time, distance and calories burnt every time you use them so that you can see how you are improving week on week.

Thirty minutes' exercise – how many calories will you burn?

As we have seen, there are several alternative ways to spend 30 minutes a day doing 'moderate-intensity' exercise to burn calories and get/keep you fit. The methods discussed on the previous pages will all help to do that.

Here is a list of the top twenty activities and the number of calories they will burn in 30 minutes (for an average person weighing 60 kilos; if you are heavier you will burn more calories). Some of these are activities that you can incorporate into your normal everyday life.

All figures are approximate.

Activity	Calories burnt in thirty minutes
Ballroom dancing	95
Golf, carrying own clubs	100
Walking, moderate (3mph)	100
Vigorous housework e.g. scrubbing	120
Horseriding at trot	120
Badminton	135
Rollerblading/skating	145
Walking, brisk (4mph)	150
Cycling, moderate (9mph)	150
Swimming, breast stroke, moderate	150
Mowing, powered, not self-propelled	165
Aerobics class, average	195
Dancing, upbeat	195
Swimming, crawl, 40 yards per minute	200
Rowing	210
Walking uphill	230
Cycling, fast (15 mph)	240
Jogging, average (6 mph)	250
Stair climbing, brisk	300
Skipping, average	335

And for the Family ...

As this book is intended for all the family, it is worth taking a few minutes to consider how we can help our children to be more active in their daily lives. As stated in the Wanless report, *Securing Good Health for the Whole Population:* 'the level of physical activity of an individual at a young age may influence the level an individual is likely to engage in throughout life.'

And the Chief Medical Officer's report, *At Least Five a Week,* concluded that all children and young people should do a minimum of 60 minutes a day of at least moderately intense activity. He also said, 'At least twice a week, this should include activities to improve bone health, muscle strength and flexibility.'

Whilst a survey shows that 75 per cent of children aged between two and fifteen do achieve an hour a day of at least moderate exercise in the UK (mostly at school, including informal activity at break times and organised PE and sports), a quarter do not – and, as children (particularly girls) get older, their activity levels tend to decline.

Interestingly, it seems that it is when 'school's out' that children's activity levels dip. One Scottish survey shows that before they begin school, small children get on average less than 30 minutes activity a day, while research from Bristol University shows that children become less active at weekends and in the school holidays. And by the time they leave school, many tend to give up sport altogether, with 70 per cent of leavers doing no sport at all.

This indicates to me that we are not doing enough to help and encourage our children to enjoy leisure activity; and we are not doing enough to ensure that they get their full quota of exercise. The lure of the TV and computer games may largely be to blame – and I suspect that many parents regard these two as unpaid childminders because of the busy lives we tend to lead.

And of course there is a natural concern for our children's safety which means we are reluctant to let them do things that were taken for granted not that many years ago. For example, few children are now allowed out on solo bike rides or are allowed to walk far to friends' houses. However, there are other ways ...

Here are some of ideas to help you achieve the activity goals for your children:

→ **Consider whether you could walk your child to school instead of using other means of transport.**

→ **For older children, consider whether they could cycle to school (perhaps accompanied by you – a good way to get your daily 30 minutes). Check whether the school has cycle facilities first.**

→ **Find out what facilities are available locally for children's activities – in many areas, much is free or very inexpensive. Ask at the local council-run sports centre. Some children enjoy team sports while others prefer to go solo; some like competition while others don't. Bear this in mind because if children don't enjoy the exercise they do, they won't continue doing it.**

→ **See what you can do together. If you are on a walking or cycling programme you can include older children; many will particularly enjoy walking sports such as orienteering or hill climbing.**

→ **For more informal activity, think of 'play' in the garden or park that all the family will enjoy – football, rounders, simple catch or other ball games, races, skipping ...**

→ **In school holidays, rope in friends who also have children to organise team games or trips to sporting venues such as dry-ski slopes, climbing walls and adventure centres.**

→ **On holiday, do more active things such as sightseeing, visits** to adventure or water parks, playing games on the beach, rather than just sunbathing, too much of which is not good for their health anyway.

→ If you have small children, start as you mean to go on. Set a limit on how many hours a day they can spend watching TV or on the computer, and stick to it.

→ Get older children to do chores in the house and garden, or car cleaning, for pocket money. Teens may be able to earn money by lawnmowing, leaf-clearing or similar for neighbours.

→ Always bear in mind that younger children will need your encouragement – and, often, help – in order to get their quota of exercise.

Toning and Flexibility

Your thirty minutes a day of structured activity as outlined on pages 234–40 is aerobic exercise – exercise that increases the fitness of your heart and lungs, and is sometimes known as cardiovascular exercise.

If you want all-round fitness, and a better body, you also need to do a small amount of **resistance** (sometimes called weight-bearing or toning) work to increase your muscle strength, endurance and tone and to improve your shape (e.g. a flatter stomach), as well as some **flexibility** work to improve your suppleness and the range of movement in your joints and back.

Depending on your chosen aerobic exercise, it may give you a certain amount of improvement in both these areas. For example, walking is a weight-bearing activity for your legs and thus your leg tone and shape will improve over time. Cycling provides resistance exercise for your legs, so it will have the same effect. Dancing and swimming offer a reasonable degree of flexibility exercise depending on the dance/stroke.

But you can't rely on your aerobic exercise to give all-round fitness. Both resistance and flexibility work are important, giving several health benefits.

Resistance work will:

→ improve your strength and ability to carry out everyday tasks
→ improve your performance in many areas
→ strengthen your bones
→ reduce the chances of injury
→ increase lean tissue and thus increase metabolic rate over-time
→ increase insulin sensitivity
→ improve your posture

Flexibility work will:

→ improve your mobility and/or help prevent decrease in mobility as you get older
→ improve your posture
→ reduce the occurrence of aches and pains
→ help to relax you

The next few pages provide you with a simple base of resistance exercises, concentrating on the stomach and upper body (as the legs will get some resistance benefit from most of the aerobic activities recommended), as well as flexibility-improving stretches. Do these at least three times a week – and use the leg stretches as cool-down stretches after any walking or cycling session too.

If you are interested in finding out more about weight-bearing exercise or flexibility, there are several good books and videos available in shops, on the internet or at the library which will take you further.

Safety and other tips

→ Exercise wearing comfortable clothing that will stretch as you move, and light, comfortable training shoes.

→ Exercise in a warm room and use an exercise mat.

→ Do not exercise too soon after a main meal.

→ Avoid exercise if you are ill.

→ Exercise at a time of day when you feel comfortable, not when you are too tired or stressed.

→ Do each movement carefully and breathe normally throughout unless the individual instructions say otherwise.

→ Begin each exercise in a good posture as described in the individual exercises.

→ Do the number of repeats and sets as stated, but if you feel fatigue or have any problems before the stated number are completed, then stop. Build up to the stated repeats and sets gradually. (A repeat is a repeat of one move; a set is a completed number of repeats, usually 10.)

→ If doing more than one set, wait 20 seconds between sets.

Resistance Exercises

Tricep dips

For: Backs of upper arms.
Start: Sit on the floor on your mat with your feet flat on the floor, knees bent and hands on the floor approx. 20cm behind you (as shown).

Finish: Bend your elbows and slowly lower your body towards the floor until your arms make a right angle as shown. Hold for one second, then slowly return to the start position.

Repeat 10 times for one set; do extra sets as you improve.

Upper back raises

For: Lower back strength.

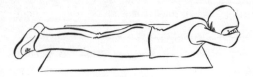

Start: Lie on your stomach on your mat with your legs out straight but relaxed. Bend your arms so that your hands are under your forehead and your elbows are out to the side on the mat.

Finish: Slowly raise your head and chest an inch or two off the mat, taking your arms with you as shown. Go as far as is comfortable; hold for one second, then slowly return to the start position.

Repeat 10 times for one set; do extra sets as you improve.

Kneeling press–ups

For: The chest and triceps (backs of upper arms).

Start: Kneel on the mat on all fours with your back straight and solid, tummy tucked in, arms level under shoulders and your hips square over your knees.

Finish: Breathe out and slowly lower your body, bending at the elbows, until your forehead is an inch or so from the mat. Breathe in and slowly return to the start position. Repeat 10 times for one set; do extra sets as you improve.

 TIP

When you get good at this, start with your knees further back to make the exercise more difficult.

Stomach 1

For: upper abdominal muscles.

Start: Lie on your back on the mat with your arms bent and fingers lightly touching your ears, and with knees bent and feet flat on the floor. Contract your abdominal muscles slightly and make sure that your lower back isn't pressed into the floor; there should be a small space between the floor and your lower spine.

Finish: Breathe out and raise your head and neck, with your arms, off the mat towards your knees, concentrating on using your abdominal muscles to achieve this, rather than your neck muscles. Raise yourself only a few inches as shown overleaf, then hold for one second and slowly lower to the start position.

Repeat 10 times for one set; do extra sets as you improve.

 TIP
For the first few weeks until your stomach muscles strengthen, you may need to have a small cushion under your head for this exercise.

Stomach 2

For: Lower abdominal muscles.
Start: Lie on your back on the mat with your arms lightly at your sides and your palms on the mat. Have your feet flat on the floor and knees bent.

Contract your abdominals slightly and raise your legs, still bent, off the mat until your thighs are at right angles to the floor as shown. Make sure you have a slight gap between the floor and your lower spine throughout this exercise – but don't arch your back.

Finish: Slowly lower your right leg a little towards the floor and as you do so, slightly bring your left leg in towards your chest. Don't allow your right foot to touch the floor. Now slowly return both legs to the start position and repeat to the other side. This counts as one move.

Repeat 10 times (10 on each leg) for one set; do extra sets as you improve.

 TIP

This exercise is quite hard – start with one or two repeats and build up.

Stomach 3

For: The waist.

Start: Lie on your back on the mat with your arms lightly on the mat near each leg, palms facing down. Have your feet flat on the floor and knees bent. Contract your abdominals slightly and make sure your lower back is in the correct position.

Finish: Slowly raise your head and upper body off the floor, raising your arms at the same time, so that they move together towards a point just to the right of your right knee.

When you have moved towards that point as far as you can go, hold for one second and slowly return to the floor. Wait for one second and repeat to the other side. This counts as one move.

Repeat 10 times for one set; do extra sets as you improve.

Stretches

It is important to stretch the muscles that you have been working to avoid injury and make them less likely to ache the day after.

The first four stretches should be done after your 30-minute structured aerobics each day (see pages 238–40 and 251–3).

The rest should be done after the resistance exercises described above.

When stretching, you should hold each position, rather than doing repeats. You will find that you can hold stretches for longer as the weeks progress.

Hamstring stretch

For: Back of thigh.
Start: Stand with your legs together, then move your right foot forward about 15cm, bend your left knee slightly and lean your body forward, placing both hands on the top of your left thigh.
Finish: As you press your hands firmly into your thigh, lift your hips and bottom up, keeping your legs still, until you feel a stretch across the back of your right thigh.
Hold for a slow count of 10.
Repeat with your left leg.

Lower calf stretch

For: Lower calf.
Start: Stand with your knees bent a little, hands lightly on your waist, your right leg about 20cm behind your left leg.

Finish: Move your body back a little so that it rests directly over the right leg, making sure to keep your right heel on the floor. Feel the stretch up your lower calf. *Hold* for a slow count of 10.
Repeat with your left leg.

Upper calf stretch

For: Upper calf.
Start: Stand with your hands lightly on your waist and, bending the left knee, step backwards approx. 40cm with your right leg (as shown).
Finish: Keeping your right heel on the floor, lean forward slightly until you feel a stretch through your upper right calf. *Hold* for a slow count of 10.
Repeat with your left leg.

Quad stretch

For: Front of thigh.
Start: Stand with your knees relaxed, legs hip width apart and arms at sides.
Finish: Bend right leg at the knee with your lower right leg behind you. Using your right hand, grab your right foot (as shown) to bring your foot in towards your right buttock until you feel the stretch up the front of your right thigh. *Hold* for a slow count of 10. Return your right foot to the floor.
Repeat with your left leg.

Back stretch

For: The spine.
Start: Stand with your knees relaxed, legs hip width apart and hands flat on each thigh.
Finish: Lean forward, curving your spine, stretching out your back and pulling in your abdomen as you do so. *Hold* for a slow count of 10.

Chest stretch

For: The chest.
Start: Stand with legs relaxed and stomach muscles contracted. Move your arms behind your lower back with your elbows slightly bent.
Finish: Bring your hands together behind your back and clasp your wrists, feeling a stretch across your chest. For a stronger stretch, move your clasped wrists out away from your body a little. *Hold* for a slow count of 10.

Shoulder stretch

For: The shoulders.
Start: Stand or sit with a straight back and stomach tucked in. Bring your right arm across the front of your body, level with your left shoulder, palm facing backwards.
Finish: Use your left palm to press your right arm firmly above the right elbow to move your right arm towards your

chest, making sure to keep the right shoulder down. Feel the stretch across your right shoulder. *Hold* for a slow count of 10. **Repeat** with your left arm.

Tricep stretch

For: The back of the upper arm.
Start: Stand or sit as in the previous stretch. Bend your right arm at the elbow and bring it upwards and backwards until your right hand hovers over your back around the level of your right shoulder, the palm facing in towards your spine.
Finish: Use your left palm to firmly press your right arm, just above the elbow, backwards until you feel a stretch through the back and side of your upper right arm. *Hold* for a slow count of 10. **Repeat** with your left arm.

Abdominal stretch

For: Stomach muscles.
Start: Lie on your stomach on the mat. Raise your upper

body off the floor, supporting your weight on your lower arms.

Finish: Raise your upper body more until you feel a stretch through your abdomen. *Hold* for a slow count of 10.

Gluteal stretch

For: Your bottom and lower back.
Start: Lie on your back on the mat with knees bent and feet flat on the floor. Place your right ankle on your left knee.
Finish: Bring your left foot off the floor and move your left leg in towards your chest. As you do so you will feel a stretch in your right buttock. *Hold* for a slow count of 10.
Repeat to the other side.

APPENDIX

BMI Instant Reckoner Chart

Weight in lbs	Height 4'10"	4'11"	5'0"	5'1"	5'2"	5'3"	5'4"	5'5"	5'6"
100	21	20	20	19	18	18	17	17	16
105	22	21	21	20	19	19	18	18	17
110	23	22	22	21	20	20	19	18	18
115	24	23	23	22	21	20	20	19	19
120	25	24	23	23	22	21	21	20	19
125	26	25	24	24	23	22	22	21	20
130	27	26	25	25	24	23	22	22	21
135	28	27	26	26	25	24	23	23	22
140	29	28	27	27	26	25	24	23	23
145	30	29	28	27	27	26	25	24	23
150	31	30	29	28	27	27	26	25	24
155	32	31	30	29	28	28	27	26	25
160	34	32	31	30	29	28	28	27	26
165	35	33	32	31	30	29	28	28	27
170	36	34	33	32	31	30	29	28	27
175	37	35	34	33	32	31	30	29	28
180	38	36	35	34	33	32	31	30	29
185	39	37	36	35	34	33	32	31	30
190	40	38	37	36	35	34	33	32	31
195	41	39	38	37	36	35	34	33	32
200	42	40	39	38	37	36	34	33	32
205	43	41	40	39	38	36	35	34	33
210	44	43	41	40	38	37	36	35	34
215	45	44	42	41	39	38	37	36	35
220	46	45	43	42	40	39	38	37	36
225	47	46	44	43	41	40	39	38	36
230	48	47	45	44	42	41	40	38	37
235	49	48	46	44	43	42	40	39	38
240	50	49	47	45	44	43	41	40	39
245	51	50	48	46	45	43	42	41	40
250	52	51	49	47	46	44	43	42	40
255	53	52	50	48	47	45	44	43	41
260	54	53	51	49	48	46	45	43	42
265	56	54	52	50	49	47	46	44	43
270	57	55	53	51	49	48	46	45	44
275	58	56	54	52	50	49	47	46	44
280	59	57	55	53	51	50	48	47	45
285	60	58	56	54	52	51	49	48	46
290	61	59	57	55	53	51	50	48	47
295	62	60	58	56	54	52	51	49	48
300	63	61	59	57	55	53	52	50	49

Find your weight (left) then move across the columns until you reach your height. The figure where weight and height meet is your BMI (see page 74).

5'7"	5'8"	5'9"	5'10"	5'11"	6'0"	6'1"	6'2"	6'3"	6'4"
16	15	15	14	14	14	13	13	13	12
16	16	16	15	15	14	14	14	13	13
17	17	16	16	15	15	15	14	14	13
18	18	17	17	16	16	15	15	14	14
19	18	18	17	17	16	16	15	15	15
20	19	18	18	17	17	17	16	16	15
20	20	19	19	18	18	17	17	16	16
21	21	20	19	19	18	18	17	17	16
22	21	21	20	20	19	19	18	18	17
23	22	21	21	20	20	19	19	18	18
24	23	22	22	21	20	20	19	19	18
24	24	23	22	22	21	20	20	19	19
25	24	24	23	22	22	21	21	20	20
26	25	24	24	23	22	22	21	21	20
27	26	25	24	24	23	22	22	21	21
27	27	26	25	24	24	23	23	22	21
28	27	27	26	25	24	24	23	23	22
29	28	27	27	26	25	24	24	23	23
30	29	28	27	27	26	25	24	24	23
31	30	29	28	27	27	26	25	24	24
31	30	30	29	28	27	26	26	25	24
32	31	30	29	29	28	27	26	26	25
33	32	31	30	29	29	28	28	27	26
34	33	32	31	30	29	28	28	27	26
35	34	33	32	31	30	29	28	28	27
35	34	33	32	31	31	30	29	28	27
36	35	34	33	32	31	30	30	29	28
37	36	35	34	33	32	31	30	29	29
38	37	36	35	34	33	32	31	30	29
38	37	36	35	34	33	32	32	31	30
39	38	37	36	35	34	33	32	31	30
40	39	38	37	36	35	34	33	32	31
41	40	38	37	36	35	34	33	33	32
42	40	39	38	37	36	35	34	33	32
42	41	40	39	38	37	36	35	34	33
43	42	41	40	38	37	36	35	34	34
44	43	41	40	39	38	37	36	35	34
45	43	42	41	40	39	38	37	36	35
46	44	43	42	41	39	38	37	36	35
46	45	44	42	41	40	39	38	37	36
47	46	44	43	42	41	40	39	38	37

For further information on these classifications see pages 74–76

Amber Portion Guide

This gives the approximate numbers of daily AMBER food portions suitable for different groups of people.

Type	Number of daily portions (approx.)
Adult Females	
Slimmers with less than three stones to lose	6 small to medium portions
Slimmers with more than three stones to lose	8 small to medium portions
Non-dieters/weight maintenance	8–9 medium portions
Adult Males	
Slimmers with less than three stones to lose	8 small to medium portions
Slimmers with more than three stones to lose	9–10 medium portions
Non-dieters/weight maintenance	10–11 medium portions
Teenagers	
Female slimmers	7–9 medium portions
Female non-slimmers	9–10 medium portions
Male slimmers	10–11 medium portions
Male non-slimmers	12 medium portions
Children aged between five and eleven	
Who need to watch their weight	6 medium portions
Who are slim or thin	8–10 portions

Fish Intake Chart

This gives the minimum and maximum weekly portion*** intakes of fish for different groups of people.

Type of fish	Women Type 1*		Women Type 2*		Girls under 16		Boys under 16		Men	
	min	max	min	max	min	max	min	max	min	max
All white fish excluding shark, marlin, swordfish	1	✗	1	✗	1	✗	1	✗	1	✗
Shark, marlin, swordfish	✗	1	AVOID		AVOID		AVOID		✗	1
Canned tuna	✗	✗	✗	4**	✗	✗	✗	✗	✗	✗
Oily fish, e.g. salmon, herring, mackerel, sardines, fresh tuna	1	4	1	2	1	2	1	4	1	4

✗ means there is no recommendation given.

* Women Type 1: Women who are not going to become pregnant in the future.

Women Type 2: Women who may have children one day,

women intending to become pregnant, and women who are pregnant or breastfeeding.

** Four medium cans. This recommendation applies to women intending to become pregnant within the next year, and to women who are already pregnant. It does not apply to women who may have children one day or to those who are breastfeeding. Note: canned tuna is not counted as an oily fish.

*** A portion of white fish is approx. 175g. A portion of oily fish is approx. 140g.

RECIPE INDEX

INDEX

Headings in **bold** type refer to exercises

The following Traffic Light food lists, which also appear on pages 31–43 in Chapter 2, can be cut out and used for easy reference (for example, when shopping).

GREEN for Go Foods

Vegetables

Artichoke, globe (fresh or canned in water); artichoke, Jerusalem; asparagus; aubergine.

Bamboo shoots; beans, broad; beans, French; beans, green; beans, runner; beansprouts; beetroot; broccoli, all types; Brussels sprouts.

Cabbage, red, white and green; cabbage, savoy; carrots; cauliflower; celeriac; celery; Chinese leaves; chicory; corn on the cob; courgettes; cucumber.

Endive; fennel; garlic; kale; leeks; lettuce, all kinds; mangetout peas; marrow; mushrooms; mustard and cress; okra; olives (fresh).

Onions, all kinds, including pickled; parsnips; peas; peppers, all colours; pumpkin; radish; rocket.

Salsify; seakale; spinach; spring greens; squash, all kinds; sugar snap peas; swede; sweetcorn kernels.

Tomatoes (fresh and canned); turnips; watercress.

Home-made vegetable soups (see recipes); home-made vegetable sauces (see recipes); commercial vegetable salsas.

Fruits

Apples, dessert or cooking; apricots; bananas, small; black-berries; blackcurrants; blueberries; cranberries; cherries; damsons; dates (fresh); figs (fresh); gooseberries; grape-fruit, grapes; greengages.

Kiwifruit; kumquats; lemons; limes; loganberries; lychees; mandarins; mangoes; medlars; melon, all kinds; nectarines; oranges.

Papaya (pawpaw); passion fruit; peaches; pears;

pineapples; plums; quinces; raspberries; satsumas; star fruit; strawberries; tangerines.

Herbs and spices

All fresh, dried or frozen herbs and spices, including chillies, garlic, ginger, basil, coriander, parsley, etc.

Dairy produce

Skimmed milk; 0 per cent fat natural fromage frais; natural low-fat bio yoghurt; soya milk and yoghurt.

Fish and seafood

All the following white (non-oily) fish:
    Cod, haddock, plaice, skate, halibut, hake, turbot, monkfish, sole; tuna canned in water (a maximum of four cans a week for women who are pregnant or intending to become pregnant; see Chapter 4, Question 22), whiting, sea bass, red snapper, hake, mullet, sea bream.

SEAFOOD:

Crab, mussels, oysters, scallops (fresh or frozen).

Pulses and vegetarian proteins

Unsweetened calcium-enriched soya milk; low-fat, low-sugar soya yoghurt; all dried pulses (cooked according to packet instructions) or pulses canned in water, including red, brown and green lentils, chickpeas, red kidney beans, soya beans, butter-beans, cannellini beans, black-eye beans; haricot beans and split peas; Quorn, including pieces, chunks and fillets; tofu, silken or firm, natural; soya mince; home-made pulse soups (see recipes).

Grains

Wheatgerm.

Condiments

Vinegar (all kinds); lemon juice; piccallili; pickled beetroot.

Miscellaneous

Tomato purée, passata, sun-dried tomatoes, sun-blush tomatoes.

Drinks

Water; red-bush tea, camomile tea, peppermint tea, lemon balm tea, and other natural unsweetened herbal teas; tomato juice; vegetable juice.

AMBER – Go Carefully Foods

Vegetables

Potatoes of all types (e.g. new, old, salad varieties), boiled or baked; sweet potatoes; yams; avocados, guacamole; olives in oil; corn canned in brine; commercial vegetable soups from the chilled counter with no added cream; all ready-made, chilled-counter vegetable sauces for pasta or cooking containing no more than 60 calories per 100ml (check the label).

Fruit

Dried fruits, including dried apricots, peaches, prunes, apples, pears, figs, dates, raisins, sultanas, currants and cranberries; rhubarb.

Dairy produce and eggs

Semi-skimmed milk; goat's milk; natural whole milk bio yoghurt; natural Greek yoghurt or half-fat Greek style yoghurt; 8 per cent fat natural fromage frais; cottage cheese; feta cheese; fresh goat's cheese; Italian mozzarella cheese; half-fat Cheddar cheese; Brie; Camembert; reduced-fat cheese sauces and dips.

Hen's eggs (boiled or poached), duck eggs, quail's eggs.

Fish and shellfish

Swordfish, shark, marlin (see Chapter 4, Question 28), and all the following oily fish, fresh or frozen:

Salmon, tuna, mackerel, trout, sardines, pilchards, sprats, herring, kipper, eel, jellied eel, carp.

Mackerel, pilchards or sardines canned in tomato sauce.

SEAFOOD:

Lobster, prawns, squid, octopus.

Meat, poultry, game

Beef – all lean cuts, including extra-lean minced beef, steak (remove fat band), lean roast beef; leg of lamb (skin removed); lamb steaks and fillet; pork fillet (tenderloin); pork steaks; leg of pork (excluding fat and skin); lean ham (reduced-salt varieties).

Chicken, all cuts (skin removed before eating); turkey, all cuts and mince; pheasant; duck meat (excluding fat and skin); guinea fowl, venison, veal, rabbit, pigeon and any other game birds; kidneys and liver (avoid if pregnant).

Offal, including liver and kidneys.

Pulses and vegetarian proteins

Baked beans in tomato sauce; ready-made hummus; TVP (textured vegetable protein) mince; soya mince; ready-made lentil pâté; ready-made mushroom pâté; ready-made hazelnut pâté; ready-made felafel patties; ready-made bean burgers; ready-made pulse soups; refried beans.

Nuts and seeds

All fresh nuts, including almonds, chestnuts, peanuts, macadamias, walnuts, brazils, hazelnuts, cashews, pecans (excluding coconut); ready-made nut roast.

All fresh seeds, including pine kernels, sunflower seeds, poppy seeds, pumpkin seeds, flaxseeds.

Grains, baked goods and cereals

Basmati brown rice, basmati white rice; bulghur wheat; rolled oats; pot barley; quinoa; traditional couscous.

Wholewheat pasta and noodles; wholewheat/wholemeal bread; oatbread; granary bread; dark rye bread; brown bread; white bread; wholewheat pitta bread, white pitta bread; chapati; flatbread.

Ready-made, shop-bought, vegetable- or fish-topped thin and crispy pizza, or home-made pizza (see recipes).

Oatcakes with no added sugar; brown rice cakes; dark rye crispbreads.

BREAKFAST CEREALS:

No added-sugar muesli; porridge, instant oat cereal; whole-wheat breakfast biscuits; Shredded Wheat; Puffed Wheat; All Bran, Bran Flakes; Cheerios; Fruit 'n' Fibre.

Fats and oils

Groundnut (peanut) oil, olive oil, sesame seed oil, walnut oil, rapeseed oil, cooking oil spray; traditional French dressing.

Miscellaneous

All shop-bought, ready-made main meals containing less than 10g fat per portion (check the label); all takeaway main meals containing less than 20g fat and 500 calories per portion.

Ready-made sandwiches containing less than 10g fat and 300 calories per portion; ready salads containing no more than 10g fat and 300 calories per portion.

Skimmed or semi-skimmed coconut milk.

Condiments

Low-salt stock cubes or bouillon; low- and reduced-fat salad dressings and sauces, including reduced-fat salad cream and mayonnaise; chutney and pickles; fruit relishes; mustard; tomato ketchup.

Snacks

Pretzels.

Drinks

Coffee; green tea, white tea, black tea, oolong tea; pure fruit smoothies made with whole fruit at home (see recipes); soda water.

RED – Stop and Think Foods

Vegetables

Chips, fried; chips, oven; chips, microwave; potato salad; olives in brine; breaded onion rings; breaded mushrooms; vegetable crispbakes; cream of vegetable soups.

Fruit

Dried banana chips; olives in brine.

Nuts and seeds

Salted nuts of any kind, e.g. salted cashews or peanuts; roasted seeds (salted or otherwise); coconut; coconut cream, full-fat coconut milk, tahini.

Dairy produce

Cream, all kinds, including half-fat; Greek yoghurt, full-fat; fruit-flavoured yoghurts (low-fat, low-calorie or full-fat, high-calorie); fruit-flavoured fromage frais; full-fat milk; goat's milk.

Eggs, any kind, fried.

CHEESES:

Cheddar; cream cheese; mascarpone; Danish Blue; Edam; Gruyère; Parmesan; processed cheese slices; Stilton and all full-fat/hard/blue cheeses; full-fat cheese sauces and dips; blue cheese dressing.

Fish and shellfish

Battered fish of any kind; deep-fried fish of any kind; tara-masalata; fish canned in oil, fish canned in brine; smoked salmon and other smoked fish, e.g. kippers.

Meat, poultry

All fatty cuts of meat, e.g. shoulder of lamb; lamb chops; pork crackling; pork spare ribs; pork chops including fat; poultry with the skin left on; beefsteak with the fat band left on; all minced beef and burgers unless labelled extra-lean; duck including fat; goose.

Sausages, all; black pudding; delicatessen cuts, including salami, chorizo, kabana, mortadella, pepperoni; bacon, all types, including ham (unless reduced-salt); scotch eggs.

Meat pâtés, all; corned beef; meat pies and pasties with pastry; ready-made, shop-bought, meat-topped pizzas.

Grains, baked goods and cereals

Any rice excluding basmati; pearl barley; white pasta; white noodles; instant couscous; polenta; pearl barley.

White rice cakes; wheat crackers of all kinds, e.g. cream crackers, water biscuits, all biscuits for cheese; cheese straws.

Flour.

Sweet biscuits, sweet snack bars, cereal bars and cookies of all kinds.

All cakes; commercial fruit pies and tarts.

All commercial savoury pies, quiches, tarts.

French bread; garlic bread; naan bread; croissants, scones, teacakes and similar.

All cereals with added sugars/honey, including corn-flakes, Frosties, Coco Pops, crunch-type baked cereal mix; chocolate-coated cereals; cereals with added chocolate/caramel.

Snacks

Potato crisps or similar potato snacks (all); all savoury snack packets except pretzels e.g. Bombay mix, tortilla chips, oriental mix; popcorn; Twiglets.

Fats and oils

Butter, margarine, blended vegetable oils, corn oil, sun-flower oil, safflower oil, dripping, lard, suet, low-fat spread.

Confectionery

All chocolate; all sweets (!), sugar; honey.

Desserts and ices

All commercial desserts and ices, including custards, mousses, instant packet desserts; jellies; flans, cheese-cakes, sponges, trifle, caramel desserts, rice pudding, meringues, roulade, chocolate puddings, eclairs; ice cream tubs; individual ice creams and lollies.

Condiments

Mayonnaise, full-fat; full-fat dressings; hollandaise sauce; peanut butter, jams; salt; soya sauce; processed meals and snacks containing more than 1.25g salt (0.5g sodium) per 100g.

Miscellaneous

All ready-made, pour-over or cook-in sauces (for pasta, meat, etc.) containing more than 60 calories per 100g (check the label); all takeaway meals e.g. Chinese, Thai, Indian, Greek, burger bar, fish and chips; pizza, deep-pan, cheese or meat; all shop-bought ready main meals containing more than 20g fat per portion (check the label).

All shop-bought ready salads, sandwiches or light meals containing more than 300 calories per portion and/or more than 10g fat per portion (check the label).

Tinned soup, packet dried soup.

Drinks

All carbonated (fizzy) soft drinks both 'diet' and original (!); all squashes and cordials (!); all ready-made 'juice drinks' (!); all fruit juices; all alcoholic drinks; all traditional and instant-type hot milk drinks, e.g. chocolate, malt; all commercial flavoured waters, both 'diet' and non-diet versions.